Marilyn Floyde has worked in performing arts and community theatre throughout her career, and has directed arts programmes around the UK. She has written plays, musicals and libretti for choral works. Recently two major cantatas have been performed and broadcast: 'Waters of Time' (composer Ronald Corp) in Wells Cathedral and the Colston Hall, Bristol, about Wells and Somerset, and a BBC Commission, 'Weaving the Future' (composer Bill Connor) in The Guild Hall, Preston, about Lancashire.

She was educated at Dartington College of Arts and has an MA in Creative Writing from University College, Chichester. She writes regularly for the website www.burgundytoday.com and has lived in France since 2000.

KING ARTHUR'S FRENCH ODYSSEY
Avallon in Burgundy

Marilyn Floyde

KING ARTHUR'S FRENCH ODYSSEY

Avallon in Burgundy

Vanguard Press

VANGUARD PAPERBACK

© Copyright 2009
Marilyn Floyde

The right of Marilyn Floyde to be identified as author of
this work has been asserted by her in accordance with the
Copyright, Designs and Patents Act 1988.

All Rights Reserved

No reproduction, copy or transmission of this publication
may be made without written permission.
No paragraph of this publication may be reproduced,
copied or transmitted save with the written permission of the publisher,
or in accordance with the provisions
of the Copyright Act 1956 (as amended).

Any person who commits any unauthorised act in relation to
this publication may be liable to criminal
prosecution and civil claims for damages.

A CIP catalogue record for this title is
available from the British Library.

ISBN 978 184386 569 8

Vanguard Press is an imprint of
Pegasus Elliot MacKenzie Publishers Ltd.
www.pegasuspublishers.com

First Published in 2009

Vanguard Press
Sheraton House Castle Park
Cambridge England

Printed & Bound in Great Britain

Dedication

To my mother, Ida Kathleen Floyde

ACKNOWLEDGEMENTS

I owe a huge debt of gratitude to Geoffrey Ashe for introducing me to Roithamus and the French 'Avalon' theory, and for continuing to give me guidance throughout the research and writing process.

Heartfelt thanks to Steph Bramwell, mentor and friend, and Pam Elson at www.burgundytoday.com for encouraging me from the outset, for reading the many incarnations of Arthur, and for severally giving me their wisdom and experience over glasses of chilled Chablis.

Grateful thanks to Françoise Garlick who undertook the first French translation, and Jean-Pierre Blivet, Karen Large, Sébastien Lebdiri, Michelle Dominique Lizieri, Marianne Mateo de Havilland, Margaret Rougeot, Margaret van den Bergh and Josie Walter who also generously read the draft, but who are by no means responsible for any mistakes or omissions.

Special thanks to John Garlick for the maps; to James Boden for the website and Will Floyde for the photographs on the website.

Thanks to everyone who spurred me on, shared their local knowledge, lent me books, and came walking around the Avallonnais with me, including:

Paul Anderson; Jamie Atkins; Christine and Graham Battye; Peter Barnes; Caroline and Martin Bean, Oreste Binczak; Mike and Barbara Bird; Blossom; Tom and Ros Colclough; Joyce Court; Rodney Davies;Patricia Deschamps; Siân Duval; Maria Dworski; Kerry Ellis; Graham Elson; Chris Ferris; Michael D Finch; André Gautherot; Cynthia Gayneau; Veronique Giarrusso; Mike Gilpin; John Goodall; Deb Goodenough; Jessica Griffiths; David and Lynne Hammond at Burgundy Discovery; Ros Hanson; Johan Klaver; Krishna Lester; Nathalie

Liamine; Yves Loiselet; Yves Loiselet; Hilary and John Longman; Sandy Maberley; Camille Maitre; Aat Mante; Phil Nadin; Elisabeth Noble; Chris Payne; Thérèse Poulain; Mike and Jenny Reed; Saffy; Pete Scholes; Sidney Sadgrove; Roger Stennett; Sue Street; Ben Sutcliffe; Rebecca Sutcliffe; Robert and Di Tring; Jonathan Trout; Kelly Whitfield; AnneMarie and John Williams; Susan Wolk; Andrew and Moira Woodhead.

Finally, thanks to Richard, Olivia and Eleanor for putting up with Arthur in the family for so long.

Thank you everyone at Vanguard Press for making this possible.

CONTENTS

ACKNOWLEDGEMENTS	11
FOREWORD	15
PREFACE	17
1 INTRODUCTION	19
2 KING ARTHUR – LEGEND AND FACT	27
3 AVALLON – WHAT'S IN A NAME?	46
4 AVALLON – THE HEALING SANCTUARY	67
5 AVALLON – THE FORGES	93
6 AVALLON – THE POETIC LANDSCAPE	113
7 AVALLON – THE FINAL RESTING PLACE	145
8 AVALLON – THE END OF THE JOURNEY?	173
APPENDIX 1	187
APPENDIX 2	194
BIBLIOGRAPHY	201
INDEX	207
ENDNOTES	214

FOREWORD

By Geoffrey Ashe

During my first long-ago explorations of the Arthurian legend, I came across references to a fifth-century British king known as Riothamus. It seemed that he led a bold but unsuccessful campaign on the continent. I noted a few scraps of information in my book From Caesar to Arthur, which was published in 1960.

It is curious that Riothamus, like Arthur, vanishes instead of dying.
After his defeat, he escapes to Burgundy, and no more is told of him.
In Burgundy, by the way, there is a town called Avallon!

Avallon or Avalon, however spelt, was of course the name of Arthur's last earthly destination, according to legend.
Gradually, with inexcusable slowness, a reason for these parallels dawned on me. "Riothamus" can be construed as a title or honorific meaning "supreme king", and perhaps this man did not simply resemble Arthur, perhaps he actually was Arthur, so far as anyone was. If so, the real town of Avallon in Burgundy acquired a new interest. I developed the idea in another book, The Discovery of King Arthur, published in 1985 and improved since.
Now, Marilyn Floyde has most gratifyingly given my notion a full-scale treatment, going far beyond anything I thought of myself. With a prodigious first-hand knowledge of the real Avallon and the country round about, she has assembled dozens of facts—historical, religious, topographical,

archaeological—and shown that when these are taken together, they suggest that the tale of Arthur's last exploits and his "passing" may well have a factual basis, in a place where no one previously looked for it.

Arthur's activities overseas have formed a major part of his official history, as first written by Geoffrey of Monmouth. Yet historical scholarship has generally ignored them. <u>King Arthur's French Odyssey</u> gives them the attention they deserve, not credulously, but intelligently. Marilyn Floyde does not try to discredit the reconstructions of Arthur's main career that are focused on Britain; she is quite willing to accept that everything may fit together. In particular, she follows up a suggestion of my own about the way in which a Burgundian end can be reconciled with the belief that the last resting-place of the king's body was Glastonbury Abbey.

Some of her speculations, I must admit, are beyond my competence, and some are outside my purview. But the overall effect of this book is very positive indeed. It is a memorable contribution to Arthurian studies. And I can imagine a unique popular guidebook based on it, attracting visitors from all over the world.

Geoffrey Ashe
Glastonbury

PREFACE

If you're a romantic and you arrive in Avallon in Burgundy, France, then one of the first questions that comes to mind is, "Has this Avallon got anything to do with King Arthur?" There's never been a satisfactory answer to that.

In 2003, a group of people belonging to the *Sociétié de Mythologie Française* was standing outside *l'église Saint-Lazare* in Avallon when the subject came up. The tour guide gave the following response:

> *" à propos de la ville d'Avallon et de l'Avalon des romans arthuriens. Rien ne rappelle explicitement la fée Morgen ou le tombeau du roi Arthur. On peut cependant faire apparaître un souvenir brouillé des légendes celtiques en examinant quelques éléments de légendes hagiographiques à la lumière de la topographie et de la toponymie locales. "*[1]

[Translation: Concerning the town of Avallon and the Avalon of Arthurian stories. There is nothing explicitly reminiscent of Morgen le Fay or the tomb of King Arthur. One could perhaps arrive at a hazy memory from Celtic legends or by examining some elements of hagiographic legends in the light of local topography and toponymy.]

Which is a high-faluting way of saying that nobody's yet found any direct evidence linking Arthur and Morgen le Fay to Avallon, but if you start investigating local legends and the lives of saints, and rambling around the countryside with a large scale map and gazetteer, you might find something.

So I set out to do that. Searching for that 'hazy memory' has been a full-time occupation for almost two years. I have found some connections, and **King Arthur's French Odyssey** is the result.

I hope that it will appeal to the Arthur enthusiast, as the only field-study into the front-running 'French Avalon' theory put forward by Geoffrey Ashe and other contemporary scholars. It might also encourage people to visit the *Morvan* and the *Avallonnais* regions of Burgundy, on quests of their own. But mostly I hope that it will allow Arthur, fabulous King of the Britons, to take his place in France, and to stride across the Burgundy landscape.

M. Floyde
Avallon 2009
marilyn-floyde@wanadoo.fr

1
INTRODUCTION

According to the earliest written texts Arthur, fabulous King of the Britons, spent a large proportion of his life in France. Was the 'Avalon' of mythology based on the *Avallon* in Burgundy?

The first person ever to mention 'Avalon' was Geoffrey of Monmouth[2]. He is the father of the Arthurian story. Geoffrey lived in Britain sometime between 1100 and 1155 AD. Avalon appears twice in connection with King Arthur in his **History of the Kings of Britain** *[3]* which he wrote in about 1136 AD. In his other work, **Vita Merlini** (The Life of Merlin, circa 1152 AD), he elaborates on Avalon as a healing sanctuary run by Morgen le Fay and her 'sisters'.

All subsequent Arthurian material, from medieval romance to 21st century film representation, pays homage to Geoffrey's writings. He is the first writer to give us a 'life' of Arthur, his ancestors and birth, his journeys and battles, his friends and foes, his beliefs and his ultimate destruction. He doesn't mention the Round Table, or the Holy Grail, or Sir Lancelot. And there are no swords in stones or ladies in lakes. Those have all been added by later writers. But Geoffrey's tales have sufficient history and magic to breathe enduring life into Arthur the legend, and to turn him into the most famous king, ever.

From Malory to Tennyson, Mark Twain to Jean Cocteau, Geoffrey's material has prompted great writers to flesh out Arthur and create new characters and whole new branches of the story. Through the ages Arthurian scholars have been writing papers, forming societies, digging up archaeological sites and debating passionately held views. Academics organise conferences and seminars and make television documentary programmes. Throughout the world students have worked their way through specialist courses, degrees and doctorates. Millions of dollars have been generated by the book and film markets. The raft of esoteric Arthuriana, the theme and backbone of tourism in many locations, has provided a living for tour operators, hotels, restaurants, pubs, shops, fairs and festivals, and an endorsement for New Age druids everywhere …

The search engine results for websites about King Arthur (21,700,000) remarkably outnumber those found for John F Kennedy, and Prince William, and outnumber those for Tony Blair, Charles de Gaulle, John Lennon, Johnny Hallyday, Princess Diana and Osama Bin Laden[4] added together. And yet it is not certain, and probably never will be, that this most famous of British kings ever existed at all.

Geoffrey of Monmouth was the first to write about Avalon, but he wasn't the first to mention Arthur. In his Dedication at the beginning of **History** Geoffrey himself says that his source material was "a certain very ancient book written in the British language." This book has never been found. He says that he received the ancient book from his friend, Walter, Archdeacon of Oxford who was "well-informed about the history of foreign countries."

So what are Geoffrey's earlier sources that we *do* know about? And do any of them shed any further light on Arthur's connections with France? Geoffrey says that he used the writings of the sixth century monk Gildas, and the historian Bede as his sources. It is said that Gildas wrote his **De Excidio Britanniae (The Ruin and Conquest of Britain**, 546 AD?) on a remote island off Brittany, which means that at least he ventured across the Channel. As far as anyone knows, Bede never left his cloisters. But in any case, neither of them mentions Arthur by name.

The oldest known document recording specifically some of Arthur's exploits, was allegedly written in 830 AD by a Welsh monk from Bangor named Nennius. It was called **Historia Brittonum.** Nennius' writing is muddled, and he is the first to cast aspersions on the reliability of his own work, calling it 'a heap of all that I have found'. He didn't refer to Arthur as a King, but he did call him a 'Dux Bellorum' – a war overlord. His big contribution was to list the twelve battles that Arthur is supposed to have fought. These battles have kept academics sparring with each other for years. None of them is easy to locate geographically, and they have all been the subject of much creative speculation. It is obvious that Geoffrey of Monmouth used Nennius as there is a close relationship between Geoffrey's and Nennius' named battles. But, there are battles which Nennius names which are not contained in Geoffrey's account, and vice versa. At least one distinguished Arthurian scholar believes that one or more of these could have taken place in France. Geoffrey Ashe[5] puts forward a theory that the battle of 'Agned' as listed in Nennius, might well be 'Angers' – a scribal corruption or abbreviation of the Latin 'Andegavum'.

The preface to the 'Legend of St. Goeznovius'[6] supposedly written in about 1019 AD by William, Chaplain to Bishop Eudo of Leon, not only mentions Arthur as a 'King' for the first time, but it also confirms his presence in Gaul:

> " ... this same Arthur after many victories which he won gloriously in Britain and Gaul, was summoned at last from human activity ..."[7]

In a landscape almost empty of any other pre-Geoffrey historical references, other early sources which may be relevant to Arthur's adventures in Gaul include the early Arthurian romances written by French authors, chief amongst them being *Chrétien de Troyes* who wrote between 1160 and 1180. Of course, being later, they may all have been based on Geoffrey. Or maybe not. Perhaps they all, Geoffrey included, drew on the old songs, legends and poems of the oral tradition of itinerant minstrels and troubadours. The use of a time machine could be the only method we'll ever find out for sure.

I've read as many local history books as I could find – despite an inadequate grasp of French. And I am more grateful than I can say to Richard Sutcliffe and Françoise Garlick for putting me straight on so many occasions. I have also read present-day commentaries and theories about Arthur – some from the outer limits of the internet where no sane person should ever go! However, the book that inspired me to take seriously the question about Arthur in Burgundy, is Geoffrey Ashe's **The Discovery of King Arthur** [8].

In **The Discovery**, Geoffrey Ashe presents the theory that the model for Geoffrey of Monmouth's King Arthur, is Riothamus, a fifth century over-king of Britain and Brittany. Riothamus was real. What's more, he was last heard of fighting in France, around *Bourges* in the Loire Valley. He was badly trounced and had to escape eastwards towards the 'Burgundians'. And if you go eastwards from *Bourges*, you get to *Avallon*.

I also discovered **La Chanson de Girart de Roussillon**[9] (about 1150 AD), an anonymous poem written contemporaneously with Geoffrey of Monmouth's **History**. This is a work classified as a *Chanson de Geste*, and part of the 'Matter of France' – a literary grouping together of all the French chivalrous medieval tales, mostly about Charlemagne. The chivalrous tales about Arthur and his knights are known as the 'Matter of Britain'. They are separate literary cycles.

The first thing that I realised about **Girart de Roussillon** was that the whole 10,000 line epic is geographically focussed on the area around *Avallon*. The *Avallonnais*. It was probably written by a monk from *Asquins,* or from *Vézelay*. The second thing that struck me was how similar it was to Geoffrey's **History.** Both works stem from a similar period and are written about the distant past, centuries before 'official history' caught up. They also share similar themes, characters, beasts, and battles, not in name, but in styles and layers of myth and meanings, despite being written in different languages. (Geoffrey's **History** was in Latin, and the various manuscripts of **Girart de Roussillon** were variously written in *langue d'oïl, langue d'oc,* or a mixture of the two with a touch of *poitevin*.) Whilst exploring the locations mentioned in the text of **Girart de Roussillon**, I realised that the Neolithic *Fontaines Salées*, a few miles from *Avallon,* and the story of the foundation of *Vézelay,* could provide a key to possible links with Arthur in Burgundy.

Most of my time has been spent physically exploring the *Avallonnais* area, visiting its ancient sites, walking its pathways, poring over maps and place-names, reading the lives of local saints, scrutinising archaeological finds, and questioning local people about legends and King Arthur. My preferred methodology was to research the place – then to go there and try to imagine what it was like in the fifth century, and measure that against what is known about Arthur, in fact and in fiction. Sometimes there was great accord between the research, the landscape and the imagining. Sometimes the landscape enhanced the research and was more evocative than I'd expected. And sometimes there was no resonance at all. If there was a very strong mismatch, I found myself questioning the original research. I didn't know what to call it other than an 'imagination crash'. That happened a few times. A photographic record to accompany the book can be found on www.kingarthursfrenchodyssey.com.

There have been many questions about Arthur since the turn of the millennium, indicating how popular (and probably inexhaustible) the subject is. For example, does the Arthur of pan-European Celtic legend and folklore stretch further back and beyond into the ancient civilisation of the Sarmatians? Who was Mary Magdalene and what was her connection with Arthur and with France? What is the nature of the Holy Grail? Did merchants and artisans, master masons and architects working on the great cathedrals, have access to arcane knowledge? Are there hidden papers and 'ancient books' yet to be discovered that will shed light on these mysteries? In the 21st century all of these questions have been asked (and answered) in a frenzy of esoteric writings. Fact and fiction. It seems that above all, a new global generation wants to believe in the fantastic.

One of the most puzzling questions, central to my decision to look for Arthur in France, was concerned with why Glastonbury had always been associated with 'Avalon'. In particular, when I'd read in so many contemporary sources that the discovery of the 'graves' of King Arthur and Guinevere at Glastonbury in 1191 was, to put it politely, a little suspicious, why had nobody investigated the alternative? Why had nobody investigated in detail the possibility of Arthur's Avalon being the *Avallon* in Burgundy?

I'm not a historian, and I have not tried to write an historical book. What I've ended up with is a kind of historical travelogue – a journey around the *Avallonnais* region of Burgundy, following a new Arthurian itinerary. It's been mostly solitary. Sometimes I would take along a friend – or someone who knew the area – but mostly I took a map, compass and two dogs. Many serious historians have devoted their lives to pursuing Arthur as he moves through the Dark Ages – just out of earshot – just out of eyeshot. The work of historians is what makes narrative authentic, and provides the rest of us with a banquet on which to feast. Historians look with a cool eye on the evidence. My eye might not be so cool. But I have not knowingly fabricated anything. Regarding King Arthur, we all have a duty to retell his story – and to make it spellbinding.

The facts are thin on the ground. Because of the lack of either written or archaeological evidence, we can't know that anything relating to King Arthur, whether in France or in Britain, is true. Unless some new document is discovered, or unless the clearly-labelled and authenticated body of Arthur is dug up, then no one can ever be certain. The best I can contribute is to flesh-out Arthur's time in Gaul by suggesting new pieces of the jigsaw, and to offer a new solution to a narrative problem that has always sat uncomfortably amongst the myths of Glastonbury.

If King Arthur existed then he came to Gaul. The purpose and point of this book is to awaken the idea of King Arthur in France, and to place him amongst the ancient forests, vineyards and Celtic springs of Burgundy.

2
KING ARTHUR – LEGEND AND FACT

THE LEGEND ACCORDING TO GEOFFREY OF MONMOUTH

The History of the Kings of Britain was written in about 1136 AD by Geoffrey of Monmouth. He is the first person to record King Arthur's life and deeds. Everything that subsequently has been written about King Arthur derives from this single, first, biographical source. **The History** was what amounted to a best-seller in its time. This then, is Geoffrey of Monmouth's story:[10]

It is the fifth century AD. Uther Pengradon, King of the Britons, engages Merlin to use a spell to transform him into an exact likeness of Gorlois, the Duke of Cornwall. Uther Pendragon sought Merlin's help because he was obsessively in love with Gorlois' beautiful wife, Ygerna. Because of this deception Pendragon was able to seduce Ygerna at Tintagel Castle in Cornwall. Arthur was conceived. Gorlois was subsequently killed in battle and Uther Pendragon married Ygerna.

At about this time Geoffrey tells us that a brilliant comet appeared and Uther Pendragon sent for Merlin again to interpret its significance. This is what he said:

"The star signifies you in person, and so does the fiery dragon beneath the star. The beam of light, which stretches towards the shore of Gaul, signifies your son, who will be a most powerful man. His dominion shall extend over all the kingdoms which the beam covers. The second ray signifies your daughter, whose sons and grandsons shall hold one after another the kingship of Britain." [11]

From the moment of his conception Arthur is identified with Gaul. Uther Pendragon's 'daughter' however, Arthur's 'sister', is the subject of some confusion in **The History**, and much contention elsewhere. In Geoffrey's other, later work, the **Vita Merlini**, he introduces Arthur's sister as Morgen, who later became Morgen le Fay. In some accounts, she is referred to as Arthur's 'half-sister', with whom he had an incestuous relationship. Mordred was the evil product of this relationship, and was therefore both Arthur's 'son', and his 'nephew'. Most importantly in Geoffrey's **History,** Mordred is his nemesis.

Geoffrey tells us that Uther Pendragon had been brought up in Brittany by King Budicius. He had been sent there together with his elder brother Ambrosius, the heir to the British throne, for his own safety. Britain had become a very dangerous place. When they were old enough, they returned to Britain to fight for their birthright. Geoffrey doesn't say anything about Arthur's upbringing. Given the later closeness between Arthur and his Breton cousin Hoël, and Arthur's probable familiarity with the language of Gaul, it is quite likely that Arthur followed in his father's footsteps and was also sent to Brittany to be brought up with his cousin. When

Hoël later becomes King of Brittany he answers to Arthur as his over-king, and becomes his most loyal and trusted ally.

In **The History** Arthur appears first as a fifteen-year-old boy, the age at which he was crowned, following Pendragon's death. The young King Arthur spent the first years of his reign putting Britain, Ireland and Scotland in order. His main enemies were the Saxons, Picts and Scots. He successfully overcame them. During this period 'Avalon' is mentioned for the very first time, ever. When Arthur was cleaning up Britain, he fought several significant and named battles. One of these was against the Saxons who had besieged what is now thought to be the town of Bath in Somerset, England. The passage describes Arthur arming himself before the battle:

"He girded on his peerless sword, called Caliburn, which was forged in the Isle of Avalon." [12]

Buoyed up by his triumphs he then decided to conquer France. He went there and joined up with his greatest ally, his cousin King Hoël of Brittany, and was victorious over Frollo, a Roman Tribune, in Paris.

Arthur then spent no less than nine years with Hoël away in France – away from Britain – away from his new queen Guinevere – putting Gaul in order. Geoffrey says that Hoël went south to Aquitaine and Gascony, and that Arthur stayed in central and eastern France, the present-day area known as Burgundy. What did he do there for all that time?

Years later when he returned to Britain covered in glory, he threw a royal party for all his noble allies at home and from abroad. But the celebrations were cut short. Arthur had to answer a new audacious challenge from Rome.

He was quick to cross the Channel again, this time with even more men, landing at *Barfleur* in Normandy, where armies from all over Gaul came to join him. On the boat he had a dream about a savage contest between a dragon and a bear. The dragon won, killing the bear, 'finally hurling its scorched body down to the ground.' This was interpreted as meaning that Arthur, the Dragon, would conquer a giant. Arthur was not convinced by this interpretation, and had a foreboding that it was connected with his struggle against the Roman Emperor. However, his first task on landing was to undertake a mercy-dash to *Mont-Saint-Michel* where he did indeed kill a rapacious and murderous giant.

He was soon on his way back to Burgundy, and the celebrated city of *Autun* where the Romans were waiting for him. This time the victory was not so easy, and many thousands were slaughtered. Arthur triumphed in the end and spent another year in Burgundy 'subduing the cities'. We have no more detail. All we know is that Arthur had planned to continue onwards to conquer Rome when bad news came from Britain. His nephew Mordred and Queen Guinevere, whom he had left jointly in charge of the kingdom, were having an affair, and Mordred had turned to the hated Saxons and invited them in to Britain.

In a fury Arthur returned home. He fought Mordred at the battle of Camblan and received a mortal wound. The last thing that Geoffrey of Monmouth tells us about him is that:

"he was carried off to the Isle of Avalon, so that his wounds might be attended to."

This is the second and final time that Avalon is mentioned in **The History**.

In his other work, **Vita Merlini** [13], Geoffrey elaborates on Arthur's demise. Merlin is talking to Morgen le Fay about her role in that last battle:

"Oh, how great was the slaughter of men and the weeping of mothers whose sons had perished there in the battle!
There also the king, struck by a mortal wound,
Abandoned his kingdom, and carried over the sea with you,
As you said before, he came to the court of maidens."

So, after his wounding Arthur was taken by his half-sister Morgen le Fay, on a sea journey to Avalon – a healing sanctuary run by women. Geoffrey tells us more about this Avalon:

> "The island of apples which men call "The Fortunate Isle" gets its name from the fact that it produces all things of itself; the fields there have no need of the ploughs of the farmers and all cultivation is lacking except what nature provides. Of its own accord it produces grain and grapes, and apple trees grow in its woods from the close-clipped grass. The ground of its own accord produces everything instead of merely grass, and people live there a hundred years or more.

"There nine sisters rule by a pleasing set of laws those who come to them from our country. She who is first of them is more skilled in the healing art, and excels her sisters in the beauty of her person. Morgen is her name, and she has learned what useful properties all the herbs contain, so that she can cure sick bodies. She also knows an art by which to change her shape, and to cleave the air on new wings like Daedalus; when she wishes she is at Brest, Chartres[14], or Pavia, and when she will she slips down from the air onto your shores. And men say that she has taught mathematics to her sisters, Moronoe, Mazoe, Gliten, Glitonea, Gliton, Tyronoe, Thitis; Thitis best known for her cither.

"Thither after the battle of Camlan we took the wounded Arthur, guided by Barinthus to whom the waters and the stars of heaven were well known. With him steering the ship we arrived there with the prince, and Morgen received us with fitting honour, and in her chamber she placed the king on a golden bed and with her own hand she uncovered his honourable wound and gazed at it for a long time. At length she said that health could be restored to him if he stayed with her for a long time and made use of her healing art. Rejoicing, therefore, we entrusted the king to her and returning spread our sails to the favouring winds."

There has never been an 'Isle of Avalon' in Britain, nor any place with a name remotely similar to 'Avalon' – island or otherwise. Yet, since 1191 AD Avalon has been associated with the town of Glastonbury in Somerset, England. Glastonbury believes itself to be the 'Isle of Avalon'. Glastonbury believes itself to be the location of the famous forge where Caliburn was made. Glastonbury believes itself to be the healing sanctuary where Arthur's wounds were tended. Above all Glastonbury believes itself to be the final resting place of King Arthur and his queen, Guinevere. Subsequently, Glastonbury has come to mean so much more through poetic, esoteric and religious connotations. Yet even these mystical attributes have an almost uncanny parallel in Burgundy.

There is a very ancient town called *Avallon* in Burgundy, France.[15] It may be that this is the Avalon which was meant by Geoffrey. It may be that all subsequent mentions of 'Avalon' in Arthurian literature down through the ages, can therefore be traced back to Burgundy. It may even be here that Arthur found his last resting place.

But surely, King Arthur is a legend? Geoffrey of Monmouth's works can't be considered to be the literal truth – so what is the relevance of where Avalon may or may not have been, when the whole thing is some sort of fabrication, little more than a fairy tale?

Well, that's the problem. The whole thing isn't quite a fabrication. Geoffrey's work is scattered with just enough elements – real people whose dates can be verified – and real places which were important fifth century cities and towns – facts in amongst the fantasy – to make us sit up and listen. There are clues to be found throughout his work that King Arthur's story did not simply come from Geoffrey's imagination. See how quick and easy it is to be drawn into the 'Did Arthur Really Exist?' argument? It's an argument that has fought its way across enough pages already, and an argument that will never be won.

There are many eminent Arthurian scholars who have spent a lifetime of research trying to throw some light on why Arthur, fabulous King of the Britons, who was so bold, brave and beguiling, does not get a significant mention in the whole canon of early medieval history sources until the 12th Century. One theory in particular champions the idea that Arthur's Avalon may have been, originally, the town of that name in France.

ARTHUR RIOTHAMUS
THE FACTS ACCORDING TO GEOFFREY ASHE

In his book, **The Discovery of King Arthur** [16], Geoffrey Ashe presents a theory that has never been effectively faulted. It's treated as the front-runner historical theory in Professor Lacy's **History of Arthurian Scholarship** (2006). It puts forward a flesh-and-blood soldier of great renown – an over-king of the British and Breton peoples, whose reputation as a fearless warrior was unsullied enough to carry the stories and interpretations that have thrilled the world for a thousand years. That soldier is called Riothamus. 'Rio' – king, 'thamus' or 'timos' – greatest or best. Therefore Riothamus was a soubriquet for 'over-king' not the man's actual name, which could well have been Arthur, or Arturius. So he could be referred to as Arthur 'Riothamus', in a similar convention to Julius 'Caesar'. Geoffrey Ashe proposes feasible dates for Arthur Riothamus based on exhaustive analyses of all the known texts. He suggests that Arthur Riothamus reigned between 454 and 470 AD. Appendix 1 is a fifth Century Timeline which marries this information with other known historical facts, and with the life of King Arthur as told by Geoffrey of Monmouth.

Riothamus was real. He lived in Britain in the middle of the fifth century AD. He led soldiers against the invading Saxons in Britain. He was much respected abroad by the leaders of the moribund Roman army, in their dwindling Empire. His fighting skills were admired by the Emperor's representative in Gaul. Riothamus was invited to Gaul to assist the Romans as they fought their last, desperate battles against the invading 'barbarians'. Riothamus is probably as close as we'll ever get to a real-life model for the legendary King Arthur.

What do we know for certain about Riothamus? He was called King of the Britons by the Roman Emperor. In 468 AD he went to France with a British army 12,000 strong. He was invited there by the Emperor to assist the Romans, and to fight alongside the Franks and Burgundians, in their war against the Visigoths invading from the south. It is recorded that Riothamus and his Britons came by sea, and was given a royal reception. Riothamus was an Over King of both Britain and Brittany – Great and Little Britain. Although he fought alongside the Franks and Burgundians as an ally of the Romans against the Visigoths, his army was not an uncouth, raggle-taggle tribe like any other 'barbarians', but a mighty force from across the sea, well-disciplined and highly regarded in Gaul.

Geoffrey of Monmouth has Arthur fighting *against* the Romans, and history has Arthur Riothamus fighting *alongside* them. This is not as contradictory as it may appear. The Franks had been changing sides throughout the century. They were the ultimate mercenary soldiers, along with other 'accepted' and familiar groups of 'barbarians'. The Romans had to cultivate barbarians to fight other barbarians, in order to ensure their continued presence in Gaul by this time. If, as it seems probable, Arthur Riothamus always fought on the same side as the Franks when he was in Gaul, then we can form an idea about his attitude to the Romans. We can also assume that he knew personally the major warriors of the time: for the Romans, Aegidius and then his son Syagrius; for the Franks, King Meroveus, his son Childeric I and possibly even his successor Clovis, who finally defeated Syagrius, and eventually became the first king, Clovis I, of France.

There were initial battles nearby against the old foe, the Saxons. They were occupying land at *Angers* and islands in the River *Loire*. With the Britons as their allies the Romans and Franks were victorious. At this point a letter was sent to Riothamus from a Gallic writer, who made something of a career out of writing to famous leaders of his time. He was called Sidonius[17], and later became bishop of *Clermont*. He wrote to Riothamus as 'King of the Britons', advising him of the laddish behaviour of some of his soldiers in the *Loire* valley and trusting that Riothamus would sort it out in his usual just and honourable way. This solid contemporary evidence not only confirms both the date and the circumstances of Arthur's presence in Gaul, but it also implies a level of friendship and past familiarity between the two. The Britons marched on up the *Loire* valley and occupied the town of *Bourges* where they waited for the coming battle against the Visigoths. They also waited for the Roman reinforcements promised by Syagrius. But treachery was afoot. The King of the Visigoths was told of the necessity to crush the Britons while they were vulnerable. He was also informed of their position. Two contemporary historians take up the story:

> "Euric, King of the Visigoths, came against them with an innumerable army, and after a long fight he routed Riotimus, King of the Britons before the Romans could join him." 470 AD Jordanes[18]

> "The Britons were expelled from Bourges by the Goths after the killing of many of them at Bourg-de-Déols." C550 AD Gregory of Tours, **History of the Franks**[19]

So this was Riothamus' last, bold battle. But, just like King Arthur, there's a question mark at the end. Jordanes gives us the last account of Riothamus:

> **"When he had lost a great part of his army, he fled with all the men he could gather together, and came to the Burgundians, a neighbouring tribe then allied to the Romans."**[20]

Riothamus was forced to flee with what was left of his men, to a place of safety – a sanctuary. He may have been wounded. He went due east into what is now Burgundy. He travelled along the Roman roads which criss-crossed this wealthy and fertile area of France. From the ancient town of *Bourges* to the ancient town of *Avallon* there is a Roman route. Throughout Gallo-Roman times this route was used extensively. By the 12th century it had become the Via

Lemovicensis, one of the main pilgrimage routes to *Saint-Jacques-de-Compostelle* beginning at *Vézelay*, through *La-Charité-sur-Loire, Bourges, Charost* and *Déols* and onwards to Spain. *Avallon* was a known Roman stronghold – a fortified central location through which passed the Via Agrippa, the main road connecting the south to the north of the country, and along which any Roman army would march.

Whilst their enemies were different (King Arthur v The Romans – Arthur Riothamus v The Visigoths) the treachery element is common to both stories. Geoffrey Ashe makes the point that even the names of the traitors in each case are too similar to be simply coincidental: King Arthur's traitor is Mordred – Arthur Riothamus' traitor is Arvandus. An historical **Chronicle of Anjou** refers to Arthur's nephew as 'Morvandus'. [21]

So, if we drew diagrams of what we know of the final journeys and battles of both Arthur Riothamus and King Arthur on two separate pieces of tracing paper, and overlaid them on a map of fifth century Gaul, then one quite astonishing fact leaps out. After their battles, their lives converge in Burgundy – and, conceivably, in Avallon.

GAUL AT THE TIME OF ARTHUR

There are very few contemporary written sources of information about Gaul in the fifth century. We have to rely mostly on what has since been dug up and dated by archaeologists. Once the Romans had gone, written records became the sole province of a few Christian clerics – mostly from a much later period because of the turmoil – who were biased, cloistered and often careless in their copying of earlier documents. Because the evidence is so sparse, it's much easier to know what Arthur *didn't* find in Gaul as suggested by the wealth of Arthurian romance written centuries later. Perhaps we should tackle those preconceptions first, and get them out of the way.

He would not have found any grand castles. He would not have found any vast cathedrals or abbeys. He would not even have found armies of jousting knights waiting to tourney with him. He would certainly not have found demure damsels in pointy hats waving their handkerchiefs at him. However appealing the notion, Arthur has nothing at all to do with the age of chivalry. Romantic gallantry, holy quests and the customs and accoutrements of medieval court life, all came into the stories much much later, when they were written down, from the 12th century onwards. They are as anachronistic to the reality of fifth century Gaul, as cellphones would be to Chaucer's pilgrims. Geoffrey of Monmouth, *Chrétien de Troyes*, and the rest, wrote about Arthur's France as a romanticisation of their own times rather than the reality of seven centuries earlier. So, when hunting for clues about Arthur in France from those sources, we must be vigilant and recognise the moments when Arthur 'goes medieval'.

Arthur would have known Gaul as the sum of its parts. Armorica – or Little Britain – an area larger than that which we now call Brittany, was to all intents and purposes, an extension of Britain. Gildas (494 – 560), an ascetic monk who sat on the tiny, barren island of *Houac* in Armorica and wrote a diatribe against the behaviour of the kings and chieftains of Britain, doesn't mention Arthur by name. His writings display a half-crazed obsession with the iniquities of the British kings. He sets a post-Roman British scene of incest and gratuitous violence ruled by ungodly kings and princes who should know better. In fact he's very coy about mentioning anyone by name, presumably because he feared repercussions. His work was called **"De Excidio Britanniae"** – The Ruin of Britain. It is a very important text. Whatever else he is, Gildas is an authentic, contemporary voice whose language and passion perhaps reflect more accurately than any other, the violence and turbulence of the times. His main contribution to our hunt for Arthur in France is his explanation of the government of both Brittany and Britain. A long association by race and kinship meant that Brittany, which had been colonised by disaffected Britons since the time of Emperor Maximus, saw itself as part of Britain rather than anything to do with Gaul. The area of Armorica in the north-west was an independent state and then included lower Normandy, Anjou, Maine and Touraine. The Kings of Brittany were 'descendants of Constantine' – legendary kinsmen of Arthur and his father Uther Pendragon. This would give Arthur a legitimate claim to the thrones of both Great and Little Britain.

The other old Roman regions of Narbonnais, Aquitaine, Neustria and Lugudonum were struggling to maintain their identities in terms of governance and administration. Moving a mighty army around this fragmentary and potentially hostile environment would not have been easy. Over such a large area, communications with both enemies and allies – also on the move – would have been very problematic.

We don't know exactly what Arthur's ships would have been like, so we have to assume that they had changed little since Julius Caesar invaded Britain. We know that Caesar needed 800 ships for five legions and 2000 cavalrymen plus their horses, to cross from Boulogne to the Kent coast. This was a vast armada – enough to force the Britons who came to meet them in their war chariots, to withdraw and consider their options. Geoffrey of Monmouth tells us that for his second campaign in Gaul, Arthur's army numbered 183,300 excluding the foot soldiers "who were not at all easy to count." Lewis Thorpe in his translation of **The History** maintains that Arthur probably would have set out from Britain for Gaul with not far short of the same number of soldiers as Caesar had – requiring a similar number of boats. These would have been sea-going sailing boats, with oars, approximately 30m long. Once across the Channel, they would have been suitable to continue up the larger navigable rivers of France. We know that the Romans always favoured water transport over road, therefore the coastal ports and river systems would have been of vital importance. To reach further inland Arthur would have needed a similar number of flat-bottomed, oar-powered barges. Archaeology has discovered that these kinds of barges were used by the Romans in the Rhineland and Low Countries.

There would have been an itinerant mob of suppliers, huntsmen and cooks following the soldiers. Way stations and taverns, if still left standing, would have offered other services and entertainments.

There were no new roads built in Gaul during the fifth century. Therefore the only routes possible for Arthur's army would have been along the existing Roman roads, along very ancient trackways or, most likely, up the rivers. There would have been forest paths wide enough to take carts serving the timber and charcoal/iron ore trades. There were paths between local villages and to and from summer pastures. Paths to larger market towns. Cliff paths and paths down to the shoreline. Paths by rivers. Paths by lakes. But none of these would have been suitable for a large marching army.

There would have been no significant landmarks other than natural land features and the mile posts, cities, towns, villas, temples, and arenas – or what was left of them – built by the Romans. There would be no church towers or spires to guide you to the next village. Defensive Roman military encampments with their ditches and ramparts – some abandoned – would have dotted the routes at significant river crossings or trade junctions. But the majority of Gaul would have been covered in forest. Keeping an army fed would have been a major consideration. Foraging in these ancient forests with their wild boar and deer would have been the main source of food – when plunder and pillage had been exhausted.

Outside the major towns and cities – which were, of course, all still known by their Roman or pre-Roman names, (there would be no Saint This Town or Saint That Village) people lived in rural farmsteads and cottages. These would be stone-built where stone was locally available – otherwise constructed of timber, lath and mud – after the British style. Arthur might have come across a tiny rural church, or chapel made out of wood or wattle, but it's unlikely.

The Romans finally left Britain to fend for itself in 410 AD. This eventually led to "The Groans of the Britons" – a letter which was sent to Gaul, to Aëtius the renowned military leader of the Western Roman Empire. The irate monk Gildas refers to it:

> "To Agitius [Aëtius], ... The barbarians drive us to the sea; the sea throws us back on the barbarians: thus two modes of death await us, we are either slain or drowned."

This national whinge cut no ice with the Romans, and they offered Britain no help. Gildas tells us that there was widespread famine and despair in Britain consequently, and that a period of pandemonium and violent civil war followed:

> "Kings were anointed, not according to God's ordinance, but such as showed themselves more cruel than the rest; and soon after, they were put to death by those who had elected them, without any inquiry into their merits, but because others still more cruel were chosen to succeed them."

Aëtius is the key military figure in Gaul at this time, and in the history of the decline of the Western Roman Empire. Later he became the victor at the definitive Battle of the Catalun (also known as the Battle of the Catalaunian Fields, Battle of Chalons) thought to be near *Troyes*, in 451. There, he defeated Attila and his Huns for the final time. By now the Romans were able to win victories only through precarious alliances with invading 'barbarians' – chiefly the Franks, Visigoths, Alans and Burgundians, who all fought with Aëtius in that battle against Attila. But any kind of unity in France at this time was short-lived. Kings and tribal chieftains made wartime alliances – only to re-group if more favourable terms were offered elsewhere. Fair-weather friends took any advantage of weakness, and the Romans – the mighty force that once dominated the whole of the western world – were falling apart. It was a looters' and pillagers' market.

The Franks had been invading Gaul on and off since the third century AD. They were a loose federation of tribes from what is now Germany and the lower Rhine. By the fifth century they had unofficially taken over Belgian Gaul. The Burgundians were also tolerated, following their defeat by the mercenary Huns who were brought in to assist Aëtius. Their king Gundahar was killed in the destruction of Worms. But the refugees were settled by Aëtius in new territory, with a new capital, Lugdunensis – present-day *Lyon*. From their new centre, the Burgundians once again spread outwards and began to establish a powerful presence throughout central and eastern Gaul. They were the tribe that gave its name to modern-day Burgundy.

The Roman army contained men from all over the Roman Empire, making a virtue out of necessity by appointing 'barbarian' battle chiefs to lead Roman forces against other 'barbarians'. This in itself is confusing. But it accounts for the ease with which the Franks and Burgundians both fought for, and against, the Romans in this turbulent century. The alliance with the Franks is also traditionally responsible for the fact that the Romans held on to the region around Paris until a decade after the fall of the Empire. The Franks finally made their move at the battle of Soissons in 486 AD, they defeated Syagrius, Aegidius' son, and his remaining Roman troops, and Gaul came under the rule of the Merovingians.

The Merovingian dynasty – half legendary itself – has acquired a mystical status which is still thriving in the 21st century. One legend claims that the father of Meroveus (traditional dates 448 – 456) the first Merovingian king and Arthur Riothamus' contemporary, was a 'Quinotaur' – half-man, half-sea cow. The Merovingians were pagan tribal chiefs, emerging from the Franks, fighting sometimes for, sometimes against the Romans. Childeric I (traditional dates 456 – 481), his successor and also contemporaneous with Arthur, fathered Clovis who defeated Syagrius and became King Clovis I – known as the first French king. Clovis converted to Christianity in 493.

In Gaul, when the Romans finally departed, things went from bad to worse. One big disadvantage of not living on an island is that barbarians could, and did, arrive unannounced on your doorstep at any time – and from any compass direction. Life under the Merovingians held, if anything, more terror than the dying days of the Empire. 'Barbarian' was the broad epithet for any gang of marauding bully-boys who, seeing the weakness of the crumbling Empire, seized the moment to make their move.

Picture a land in turmoil. The migration of powerful, dominant and violent tribes into Gaul bringing their own languages, beliefs and ethnicity heralded a time of great transition. The most significant areas of human concern were changing beyond all recognition: governance, language, culture, ethnicity and religion. The old world was being challenged by the new. Whether in Britain or Gaul, Arthur and his contemporaries were on the cusp of a new civilisation.

3
AVALLON – WHAT'S IN A NAME?

There are many aspects of King Arthur's story that cause controversy. Oddly enough, the one that doesn't attract very much impassioned debate is 'Avalon' – the location of the famous forge, the healing sanctuary of Morgen le Fay, and the name of Arthur's last resting place, according to Geoffrey of Monmouth.

For example, few historians question 'Avalon' in the vigorous way that they question the 'real' location of Camelot, or the location of Arthur's battles, Arthur's birthplace, Arthur's parentage, Arthur's ethnicity, Arthur's genealogy, and most vehemently, his very existence. They ask, 'Where is Camelot?', but often, when it comes to Avalon, the question is framed differently, and they ask, 'What is Avalon?' And so we get the answers that we always get – the answers that have been widely accepted since the end of the 12th century – the answers on which Glastonbury has built its name.

> Avalon is a Celtic otherworld – similar to Christian heaven or classical arcadia. It is a western nirvana – the attainment of a higher state of being – a place from where re-incarnation is possible. It is a mythical paradise – the Isle of Apples – the Welsh/Celtic Yniswitrin.

Since the 12th century 'Avalon' has been establishing itself both as a Concept and as the alter-ego of Glastonbury.

So, the question 'Where is Avalon?' has hardly ever been asked because Glastonbury, as a physical embodiment of Concept Avalon, has never been seriously challenged. Visit Glastonbury today and marvel at the range of 'Avalon' commercial services: used cars, furniture stores, B&B, grocers, cafés, fisheries, a radio station, a caravan park and so on.

It remains that there was not, and never has been as far as anyone can discover, a time when Glastonbury was known historically or geographically as 'The Isle of Avalon' until after Geoffrey of Monmouth's death. Geoffrey of Monmouth would have known all about Glastonbury Abbey. He was an ordained priest, and Glastonbury Abbey was the second richest abbey in the country. If Geoffrey meant to say that Arthur ended up in Glastonbury why didn't he say so? Where did 'Avalon' come from?

In some contemporary books when writers reach Arthur's final journey, they often mention in passing that there is an *Avallon* in Burgundy. But there they usually stop – leaving behind, with an almost Gallic shrug, a large question mark. One writer does grasp the nettle. Geoffrey Ashe[22] suggests that *Avallon* in Burgundy is a strong candidate for the location where the real Arthur sought sanctuary after his final known battle. My job was therefore made clear.

I set out to measure the present-day town of *Avallon* and the surrounding area, against both the historical facts known about Arthur Riothamus, over-king of the Britons, as championed by Geoffrey Ashe, and against the legendary King Arthur as originally 'created' by Geoffrey of Monmouth.

The convergence of legend and fact in 470 AD in Burgundy, is the conclusion of the Arthur narrative in both cases. There is, of course, no absolute full-stop at *Avallon* – in either fact or legend. The enduring fascination with King Arthur is this question mark – Arthur's alleged immortality. When no one, in fact or legend, is recorded as witnessing his death, then the narrative conclusion is full of potency and potential. Arthur Riothamus, mercenary soldier and over-king of the Britons, probably died in *Avallon*, Burgundy. Fabulous King Arthur, the once and future king, lies in 'Avalon', waiting to return to lead his country in its hour of greatest need. Is it possible that Arthur's grave could still be found in Burgundy?

AVALLON, BURGUNDY

Avallon is a town in the present day French *département* of the *Yonne* – named after the River *Yonne* which is a tributary of the *Seine*, and one of the four departments making up the region of Burgundy in eastern central France. Burgundy gets its name from the pre-Roman Celtic tribe most closely associated with the area, the Burgundians. Other significant and influential tribes in the area were the *Aedui* and the *Sequani*.

Avallon is practically in the centre of Burgundy and was an important Celtic *Aeduan* settlement with its own mint. There are coins dating back to pre-Christian times. These have a long-haired warrior on one side with the word *ABALLO*, and a horse on the other. It is widely recognised that the warriors from *Avallon* joined forces with *Vercingetorix* and the other Celtic tribes in the final battle against Caesar close by, at *Alésia*.

Avallon is also a gateway town to the *Morvan* which is a wild, mountainous granite upland in the heart of Burgundy. In Roman times *Avallon* and the surrounding area was a known summer resort for wealthy Romans and their families[23]. The countryside is verdant and fertile, with cherry and apple orchards in the valleys, and vineyards on the chalky escarpment. The immediate environs, known as the *Avallonnais,* resonate with ancient history.

The area has seen continuous habitation since the beginning. People from every stage of human development, from Cro Magnon to Homo Sapiens, have lived in the valley of the River Cure – that magical river whose very name suggests its place in Celtic mythology.

The origins of Avallon are very ancient. One source claims:

> *"On peut donc dire qu'il est peu de villes dont l'ancienneté d'origine soit mieux établie que celle d'Avallon."*[24]
>
> [Translation: We can say, therefore, that there are few towns with better ancient credentials than those of Avallon.]

There existed a Celtic *'collège de Druides'* which later, under the Romans, became the school for which *Avallon* was known throughout Burgundy. It is thought that *St. Germain* (Germanus, Bishop of *Auxerre* as mentioned in Geoffrey of Monmouth's *History*), who would have been a near contemporary of Arthur Riothamus, went to school there.

Because of its position high on a promontory *Avallon* has good natural defences. This was essential as it was continuously vulnerable to attack. It was an important way station on the main north-south Roman road – the Via Agrippa *(Boulogne* to *Lyon)* – which, during the unsettled post-Roman era, meant that it frequently became the site of battles, sieges and bombardments from all manner of marauding 'barbarians'. The promontory and ramparts are bordered by two tributaries of the River *Cousin* and a stream. These are only shallow now (due to water-flow controls from the man-made *Morvan* lakes) but there are records which indicate serious flooding in the 17th and 18th centuries. Similar to Glastonbury, it could once have been an island from time to time. Other Roman roads linked *Avallon* with *Alésia, Autun* (Augustodonum), *Sens* (Agedincum), and *Paris* (Lutèce). Significant to our story though, is the Roman road which directly linked Avallon with the '*agglomération*' of *Les Fontaines Salées* [25] and *Bourges* to the west.

Today there's not much left of the ancient *Avallon*. The place is an elegantly faded 19th century market town – except for the old quarter and the ramparts which are reached by walking up the narrow cobbled street from the Mairie towards the clock tower. Everything changes then. You can see the true medieval nature of the architecture. Both the Museum and the Tourist Office are here. Going underneath the clock tower you find the *Eglise St. Lazare* on the other side – the oldest church in Avallon – but still nowhere near old enough for King Arthur. It has the most wonderful zodiac doorway with unique barley-sugar *collones* or pillars – and inside it's dark and mysterious. There's always plainsong and Gregorian chanting. For a minute you imagine that you've walked in on choir practice, but it's, sadly, all electronic. I suppose that the CDs set to continuous random play, have replaced the medieval choristers employed to sing the psalms in perpetuity. It was founded on the site of an earlier church in about 800 AD. Legend has it that *Avallon* achieved prime pilgrimage status because of the bones of St Lazarus (he who was brought back from the dead) provided by Girart de Roussillon, who also endowed *Vézelay* with the relics of Mary Magdalene, Lazarus' sister. His bones however, caused an evil little spat with the diocese of *Autun*, which claimed it had the real ones…

If you walk down the alley to the left of the church you will find yourself out on the ramparts which are very impressive. Look out across the *Morvan*, it's a view that conceivably Arthur would recognise. If you take the lower road out of the town, down past the ramparts, you can see the very pretty terraced gardens underneath the town fortifications.

This route will also lead you to the valley of the *River Cousin*, where it's worth parking your car, crossing the river over the little footbridge, and walking along the river bank. If it's a sunny day the shallow water bubbles and sparkles over the smooth rocks. And it's altogether joyful.

There is no point in wasting any time agonising over the spelling of *Avallon* in Burgundy. Throughout the centuries there has been an easy carelessness about that extra 'L'. On Peutinger's Map of 1264 it is marked as the Latin 'Aballo'.

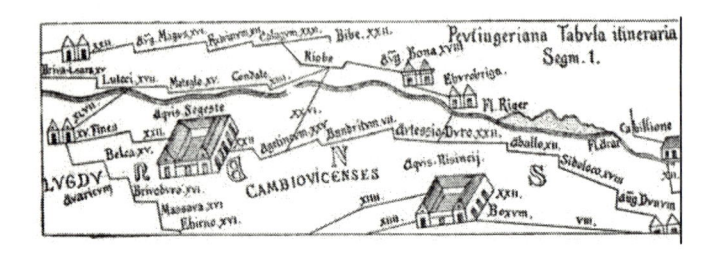

From an early 1610 print, the name *'Avalon'* can be clearly seen. There are many other examples of the single 'L' spelling from the eighteenth century, but by the late nineteenth century it had settled down as *'Avallon'*. To avoid any confusion, I'll use *'Avallon'* to mean the town in Burgundy throughout.

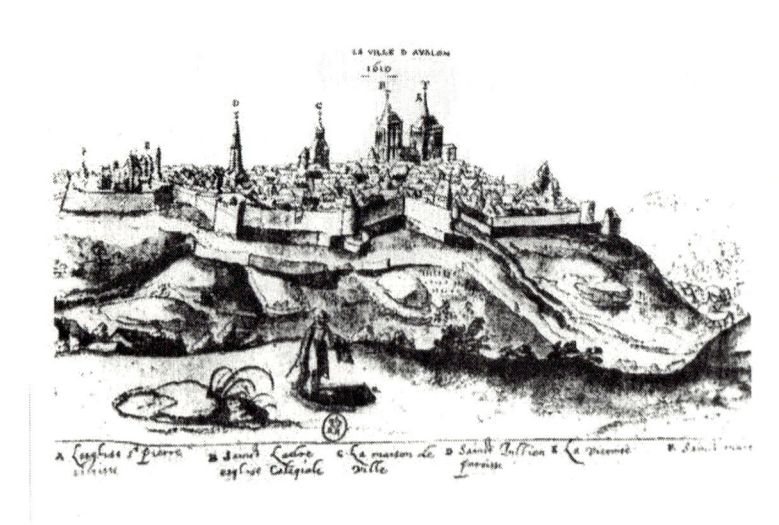

'Avalon' and 'Avallon' both came from the same root, and originated with exactly the same meaning. The name *Avallon* means 'apple'.

From "**Avallon Ancien et Moderne**" by A. Heurley first published 1880:

> [On the derivation of the name '*Avallon*'] *"Son nom, d'après certains historiens, viendrait d'un mot celtique, Avaleum, qui signifie pomme. Cette opinion paraît appuyée sur ce qu'une petite île d'Angleterre, où il croit beaucoup de pommiers, s'appelle encore Avalonia."*[26]
>
> [Translation] The name, according to certain historians, comes from a Celtic word, Avaleum, which means apple. <u>**This opinion appears to be based on the fact that a small island in England where a lot of apple trees grow, is still called Avalonia.**</u> (my emphasis)

Here then is *Avallon's* first step on the slippery slope to Arthurian obscurity. One of the very first history books about *Avallon* (above) mentions that there is a small island in England called Avalonia – putting *Avallon* in second place, almost as if it is embarrassed about its credentials. *Avallon* as a town almost certainly pre-dates Glastonbury, and so far as any ancient location is concerned, it is the only *Avallon* in existence. At the risk of repetition, there is no Avalonia in England famous or otherwise for its apples. There is no island of that name, or anything like it, in England. There never has been.

53

This French history book reflects exactly an attitude prevalent amongst the local people I have interviewed about the name of their town, and its Arthurian associations. They say that *Avallon* has the same name as the place in England, and was probably named after it. 'There's no Arthurian connection as far as we know to our *Avallon* – it's just a coincidence that we have the same name,' they say. So, even amongst its own inhabitants there's a long tradition of ignoring the obvious.

Avallon, Burgundy, doesn't ring any Arthurian bells because since the earliest times, the people of *Avallon* have been told that their *Avallon* isn't in the running – that there's a kind of *appellation contrôlée* over the world-famous Avalon of King Arthur – and it belongs to England. Is it possible that the reverse might be true? That all of the mentions of Avalon in the canon of Arthurian literature, may originally have derived from the *Avallon* in Burgundy? From a dim recollection of the place where Arthur Riothamus sought sanctuary from the Visigoths?

Is it possible that Avallon, Burgundy, has missed out on a thousand years of potential tourist income because of a few opportunistic monks in England in the 12th century?

So, we now have to look at why the *Avallon*/Burgundy/Arthur connection has been largely ignored until now. Who were these English monks who had such power and influence that they managed to hoodwink Christendom for hundreds of years?

Well, hoodwinking large numbers of people with miraculous body parts and artefacts was the stock-in-trade for medieval monks. Europe was rattling with old bones and relics, and the coffers of the abbeys and monasteries were overflowing with taxes from the mills and wine-presses, with harvest levies, tithes and fees from the stalls at the Fairs on Holy Days. But the most lucrative activity was the Pilgrimage. It was a little gold mine. The Pilgrimage brought the very best of everything to the Abbeys. Hordes of people spending money on food and accommodation and buying official keepsakes and mementoes; old and sick people buying pardons and privileges; people scared out of their wits by demons and damnation buying Masses and doing expensive penances to save their eternal souls; guilty 'sinners' leaving lands and chattels to the already rich institutions ... The competition – Europe-wide – for the best Pilgrimage was as tough then as it is now for the top tourist attractions. There were no holds barred. It was an abbot-eat-abbot culture, and may the best old relic win. This is one of those times when the story of Arthur goes medieval – and how. As we shall see, in 1191 Glastonbury hijacked the name 'Avalon' and made it its own.

THE GLASTONBURY CLAIM

Something very significant happened in 1191. The Glastonbury monks dug up King Arthur and Queen Guinevere in Glastonbury Abbey's cemetery. We all know it was King Arthur and Guinevere because there was a lead cross buried in the tomb, which said it was them. There were 'two stone pyramids' which marked the spot.

Gerald of Wales 1146-1223 [Giraldus Cambrensis in Latin] was an eyewitness. He is the first to equate the name

'Avalon' with Glastonbury. He mentions the discovery of the tomb in detail in two of his works which can be read in full on the excellent Camelot Project website at www.library.rochester.edu/camelot/gerald.htm. Concerning the cross he says:

> "A lead cross was placed under the stone, not above as is usual in our times, but instead fastened to the underside. I have seen this cross, and have traced the engraved letters -- not visible and facing outward, but rather turned inwardly toward the stone. It read: "Here lies entombed King Arthur, with Guenevere his second wife, on the Isle of Avalon."

He also says that King Arthur's bones were huge ... Gerald writes in a peculiarly defensive style. Has he been told what to write and is feeling uncomfortable about it?

That this was, indeed, the grave of King Arthur and Guinevere has been hotly debated by Arthurian scholars. In his book, **The Discovery of King Arthur**, Geoffrey Ashe says, "Most modern authors (not all) reject the discovery as a fake." He goes on to talk about relative fakery. He himself was an eyewitness to the re-excavation of the site in 1963 by Ralegh Radford which at least proved that there had been an old grave where the monks said there was. He also offers several suggestions about what the monks didn't claim they'd found (the Grail, for example), as an indication that fakery wasn't perhaps as widespread as supporters of the hoax theory might imagine. But none of that answers the question as to who was buried there, or why the monks started digging where they did in the first place. And why on earth should the grave contain Guinevere when according to Geoffrey of Monmouth she had betrayed Arthur with Mordred?

Gerald's explanation as to why Glastonbury is called 'Avalon' also exhibits the contorted style of a man trying very hard to convince others of facts which he doesn't entirely believe himself: (All of Gerald's words are taken from his accounts exactly as translated by John William Sutton for The Camelot Project).

Gerald says:

"What is now called Glastonbury was, in antiquity, called the Isle of Avalon; it is like an island because it is entirely hemmed in by swamps. In British it is called Inis Avalon, that is, insula pomifera. This is because the apple, which is called aval in the British tongue, was once abundant in that place. Morgen, a noble matron, mistress and patroness of those regions, and also King Arthur's kinswoman by blood, brought Arthur to the island now called Glastonbury for the healing of his wounds after the Battle of Camlann. Moreover, the island had once been called in British Inis Gutrin, that is, insula vitrea; from this name, the invading Saxons afterwards called this place Glastingeburi, for glas in their language means vitrum, and buri stands for castrum or civitas."

He goes on:

"Truly it is called Avalon, either …because apples and apple trees abound in that place; or, from the name Vallo, once the ruler of that territory…"

(No one has managed to place Vallo …)

And on:

"Likewise, Insula Vitrea … evidently on account of the river, most like glass in colour, that flows around the marshes. It is clear from this, therefore, why it was called an island, why it was called Avalon, and why it was called Glastonia;"

As clear as mud from the River Brue, Gerald. As to the 'lead cross', well, given that a very old grave was discovered last century on the site, the cross is the only clue as to its contents. Gerald wasn't the only witness. The cross itself was seen by many reliable people up until its disappearance in the early 18th century, last heard of in the possession of a Mr. William Hughes, Chancellor of Wells. Which doesn't, of course, preclude the fact that it was possibly a forgery right from the start. There was Ralph of Coggeshall in 1225, Adam of Domerham in 1291, the monks of St Albans sometime in the 13th century, the monks of Margam Abbey, and John Leland in 1542 who all chronicled their sighting and quoted the inscription. William Camden in 1607 helpfully made a sketch which has enabled wrangling scholars to dispute the authenticity of the Latin lettering which some maintain comes from a period much later than the fifth century.

The inscription on the illustrated cross translates as: "Here lies buried the renowned King Arthur in the Isle of Avalon". There's no mention of Guinevere – but then she could have been on the reverse side ... The witnesses didn't all agree on the exact wording, either. But there are three elements which are common to all:

King Arthur   burial   Avalon

Then, for centuries after, the famous syllogism that's duped pilgrims, holiday-makers, and the French, was born:

Arthur's last resting place is Avalon

Arthur's grave was discovered in Glastonbury

Q.E.D. Glastonbury is Avalon.

Gerald's world was a world of dualities and confusion. According to him there were two islands: *Inis Avalon* and *Inis Gutrin* named variously because of the apple trees, the waterlogged land, the name of a lord whom no one has traced, and the colour of a river. They became one place and were re-named 'Glastonbury' by the conquering Saxons. Gerald was writing about an era that was as remote from him then, as writing about Christopher Columbus without the aid of history books, would be for us today. So he can be forgiven for his confusion. Especially if none other than the king of England had taken him on one side and encouraged him to be creative with the truth.

The hoax school of thought maintains that there are plausible reasons why the powers that be should have wanted to perpetrate a fraud.

King Henry II of England (1133 – 89) – Henry Plantagenet – who could well have masterminded the plot (although he died before it came to fruition), saw himself as a bit of an Arthur. With his extraordinarily wealthy and experienced wife, Eleanor of Aquitaine, he became supremely powerful by the time he was 19, and during the first twenty years of his reign expanded his kingdom in France and became King of England. Geoffrey of Monmouth's **History** was an immensely popular book at Henry's Court, and perhaps Henry recognised that if he became instrumental in the recovery of King Arthur's body he might regain some of his former glory following the catastrophic murder of Thomas Becket. It was Henry Plantagenet that started the search by letting it be known that he had been advised (by 'poets' or 'wise men') that Arthur's body would be found beneath the pyramids.

King Arthur was a political hot potato in the 12th century. The extant writings of Geoffrey of Monmouth, and the French writer Wace, suggest an uncertainty surrounding Arthur's death and speculate about his triumphant return. Finding the body of King Arthur would provide incontrovertible evidence to the Welsh nation that Arthur was good and dead, and that he was not about to return to lead their resistance to the conquerors.

For the Abbey, finding the bones of the most successful and revered King in history would provide them with a top-flight pilgrimage shrine at a time when they were in dire need of additional funds. The rich pickings to be had from the pilgrims who would flock to see them would go towards repairing the Abbey church which had burned down a few years before, on St. Urban's Day. King Arthur's remains were the last in a long line of 'discoveries' at Glastonbury during this time. Others included the bones of Saint Patrick, Saint Brigit, Saint Gildas, and Saint Dunstan[27].

In any event, the vested interests of both Glastonbury Abbey and Henry Plantagenet were well-served by the 'discovery'.

Finally, returning to the idea of relative fakery, for the sake of the argument let's imagine that by 1191 the grave discovered at Glastonbury could have contained the remains of King Arthur (and another?). If the French 'Avalon' theory stands up, then the question is that if Arthur was originally buried in Avallon, Burgundy, how did his body get back to Glastonbury? And when?

THE FRENCH EVIDENCE

The date of the discovery, 1191, is very significant. Geoffrey of Monmouth wrote his **History** in 1136 – or thereabouts. It certainly pre-dated the discovery of King Arthur's grave in Glastonbury. Geoffrey had written what amounted to a best-seller in his day. By the time the discovery was made, everybody would have known the famous story of King Arthur. Geoffrey is the first person to mention Avalon in connection with Arthur's final destination. Again, this is what he says:

"he was carried off to the Isle of Avalon, so that his wounds might be attended to."

What did Geoffrey of Monmouth really mean by his Avalon? He says, with utmost simplicity, that Arthur was taken to Avalon for medical treatment. Arthur is not dead, he is wounded. Surely it would be premature to dispatch him from this earth to Concept Avalon? Also, the question has to be asked, that if Geoffrey, who paints a devoutly Christian portrait of King Arthur, meant Avalon to be a Celtic paradise as opposed to a real place, why on earth did he have his Christian Arthur ending up in this pagan otherworld? And not ending up in Christian Heaven? Of course, Geoffrey is no historian. He writes a fantastic melange of myth and fiction spattered with real-life people and places. Having said that, even if his whole Avalon episode were simply fantasy and based on nothing but classical allusion, then there is a massive coincidence with the factual material relating to Arthur Riothamus. It would have been very simple for Geoffrey to have said that King Arthur was buried in Glastonbury. But he didn't.

Geoffrey may have been the first, but he wasn't the only one to mention 'Avalon' in early Arthurian literature. The earlier we can go back, the more likely we are to find someone who used the same – or different – source material to Geoffrey. Like an upside down pyramid, the stories of Arthur are all based on the scantiest evidence – and the earliest writers all mention older sources which are now lost. French writers are particularly interesting on this.

12th century *Chrétien de Troyes* who gave us Sir Lancelot and the first Grail story, certainly knew the difference between his 'Avalon' and his 'Inis Gutrin'. He claimed to have been given his source, 'the book', by Count Philip of Flanders. *Chrétien de Troyes* wrote his **Erec and Enide**, in about 1170. In the story (which of course is only a story, but that's not the point) he listed the guests at their wedding. They included both Lord Moloas who was:

"a powerful baron and Lord of the Isle of Glass." and

"Guingamar ... Lord of the Isle of Avalon. Of him we have heard tell that he was the friend of Morgen la Fay, and it was the proven truth."[28]

Two Lords. Two separate places. *Chrétien* understood that the 'Isle of Glass' and the 'Isle of Avalon' were separate and different. And he should know – coming from *Troyes* – just up the road from *Avallon* in Burgundy.

Another Burgundian, *Robert de Boron*, writing in the mid -1180s refers to his source as 'a high book'. Robert was the first writer to add the sword in the stone episode. He wrote in verse. Three of his works survive and the death of Arthur comes in **Perceval**:

> "They gathered about Arthur, grieving bitterly, but he said to them, 'Stop this grieving, for I shall not die. I shall be carried to Avalon, where my wounds will be tended by my sister Morgen."[29]

In his **Joseph of Arimathea** Robert also refers to Avalon as "the Vales of Avalon" rather than the 'Isle of Avalon'. The Avallonnais region in Burgundy would be known as the 'vales' because of the four river valleys, the *Yonne*, *Cure, Serein* and *Cousin*.

From the **Modena**, or *Didot Perceval* manuscript, believed to be a prose version of *Robert de Boron* written in about 1200, Avalon also comes across as a real location:

> "And also King Arthur was wounded mortally, for he was pierced through the breast with a lance, and then they made great mourning around Arthur. And Arthur told them: "Cease your mourning for I shall not die. I shall have myself borne to Avalon that my wounds may be tended by Morgain, my sister."[30]

In his **Roman de Brut** written in about 1155, *Wace* was the first to mention The Round Table. *Wace* was a Frenchman born in Jersey and brought up in *Caen,* Normandy. He says that he uses sources independent of Geoffrey. This is how he deals with it:

"Arthur himself was wounded in his body to the death. He caused him to be borne to Avalon for the searching of his hurts. He is yet in Avalon, awaited of the Britons; for as they say and deem he will return from whence he went and live again. Master Wace, the writer of this book, cannot add more to this matter of his end than was spoken by Merlin the prophet. Merlin said of Arthur – if I read aright – that his end should be hidden in doubtfulness."[31]

In all these examples the only lack of agreement is in the nature of Avalon's geography. Was it an Isle or a Vale? Is it a town or a place name? One thing's certain – none of these early examples make so much as a passing nod at Concept Avalon. It is considered by all to be a real place.

Wace also reiterates the provenance of Arthur's sword:

"It was forged in the Isle of Avalon, and he who brandished it naked in his hand deemed himself to be a happy man."

So, as far as the name 'Avalon' goes, perhaps it's time to consider a new syllogism:

Arthur was last recorded in Avalon in the fifth century

The only location then known as Avalon was in Burgundy

Q.E.D. King Arthur's Avalon is in Burgundy, France

Knowing that Arthur has been placed in the only known *Avalon*, which is in Burgundy, by the earliest and most important English and French Arthurian sources, should give us all pause for thought.

If all mention of 'Avalon' in the canon of Arthurian literature originally came from a dim recollection of the place where Arthur Riothamus sought sanctuary from the Visigoths, then we should expect to find more astonishing co-incidences. There are. Many more.

4
AVALLON – THE HEALING SANCTUARY

THE RETREAT FROM BOURGES

In 470 AD Arthur Riothamus, and what was left of his battle-weary troops, made their escape from *Bourges* (Avaricum), after their defeat by the invading Visigoths. They went east towards the Burgundians who were known to be allied to the Romans. There were still Roman strongholds in *Avallon* and *Autun*. The Romans under Syagrius had promised him reinforcements, but they had never materialised in *Bourges*, and Arthur Riothamus and his army had been left to fight the Visigoths alone, with disastrous consequences. The Burgundians would have offered him a safe haven. Along the Roman road to *Avallon* he would have passed through some of the most beautiful landscape in France. He would have reached the '*Avallonnais*' region, surrounding *Avallon* itself, and the famous and sacred phenomenon for which *Avallon* was known throughout Gaul at that time, *Les Fontaines Salées* – literally, 'the salt springs'.

If we go now from fact, to Geoffrey of Monmouth's fictionalised **History**, he tells us that King Arthur spent two periods of time in Gaul. The first one lasted nine years during which time Arthur was in northern and central France whilst his cousin, Hoël took his armies south. The second and final campaign was shorter, but after a brief foray to *Mont-St-*

Michel where he killed a rapacious giant, he marched his army through central France, into what is now Burgundy. First he fought and defeated the Romans in a battle near *Autun*, (some 80 kilometres on a direct route south-east from *Avallon*) with massed armies from Britain and France under his command. Then he stayed in Burgundy for about a year 'subduing' the towns and cities. On the legendary side then, Arthur would have known the area extremely well as he had chosen to live there for two periods of his life which amounted to ten or more years.

Arthur Riothamus would have known the area either by repute, or by first-hand experience. Historical evidence suggests that he had most certainly been to Gaul before. He was on familiar terms with Aegidius, the General who ruled northern Gaul and established Soissons as his base. Later, it was Aegidius' son, Syagrius, who so tragically failed to deliver reinforcements.[32] We've already mentioned the letter from Sidonius about his soldiers' behaviour, which suggests that Sidonius also knew him well.

The main north-south Roman road, the Via Agrippa, follows the route from *Sens* (Agedincum), through *Auxerre* (Autessiodurum), straight through *Avallon* and on to *Autun* (Augustodunum). *Avallon* was also an intersection for a web of more minor roads reaching throughout Burgundy to important Gallo Roman towns. If Arthur Riothamus already knew *Avallon* then he would have known *Les Fontaines Salées*. And if he knew *Les Fontaines Salées*, after his retreat from *Bourges*, he would have taken his stricken men there. He would have gone there himself to be cured of his wounds.

On the banks of the River *Cure, Les Fontaines Salées* had been an important Roman spa since the first century AD, and as the name suggests, the source of mineral deposits.

But before the Romans – even before the Celts – going back to Neolithic times – the miraculous springs were also a source of great wonder. They were an ancient place of worship, and one of the most important healing sanctuaries in Gaul.

> *"Depuis des temps immémoriaux les sources ont été sacralisées. Les Gaulois croyaient que les divinités qui les fréquentaient avaient le pouvoir de guérir les malades"*[33]
> [Translation: Since time immemorial the springs have been sacred. The Gauls knew that the divinities that frequented them had the power to heal the sick.]

Les Fontaine Salées contained two open-air temples, a necropolis, and wells of salt water connected by large oak 'pipes' made from tree trunks which had been hollowed out by fire. These have been carbon-dated to around 3000 BC. For thousands of years the whole site has been used for a variety of purposes. It was a cemetery dating from about 900 BC containing ceramic funerary urns. In addition to being a healing sanctuary and a sacred place of worship, the wells provided water with a high concentration of salt which was collected and processed by evaporation. As well as being used to preserve foodstuffs, salt was used in large quantities in tanning animal hides.

The wells contain sodium, chlorine, sulphur, chalk, magnesium, iron, potassium, lithium and copper. According to an article in *Horizon* 1990 this cocktail of elements and minerals would have been particularly soothing when used as a poultice for burns[34] and flesh wounds.

But perhaps what has always given the wells their mystery and 'magical' edge, is that the springs are slightly radioactive and, from deep underground, they simmer and seethe with large, lazy bubbles of the gas helium which float to the surface.

The Romans built on to the site incorporating some elements of the existing walls and buildings. Essentially from the second century AD, and in its Roman heyday, by all accounts *Les Fontaines Salées* became a most magnificent and luxurious example of a Roman spa, with hot and cold baths, gymnasium, wrestling arena, and beauty parlour. So the site played host to yet another function – the cleansing and pampering of the body.

The wells were enclosed by a vast circular wall some three meters high with a diameter of about 30m and circumference of 94m. It is thought that this structure represented a giant wheel – in itself a symbol of the sun or moon. The Romans would have immediately recognised this as a symbol of Dispater. Caesar wrote, "*All Gauls assert they are descended from Dispater, their progenitor.*" The Celts called him Taranis – the 'thunderer' – the god of the dead – the ancestor deity. Local place-names would seem to back this up. There is a "Crot de Tarnasse" or 'Taranis' hole' a few kilometres away near *Pierre Perthuis*.[35] Small wheel-shaped fibulae or brooches were found in the confines of the temple. Diana, the Romanised consort of Taranis, was a goddess closely associated with the moon and was the protector of women, especially in childbirth. She was also a goddess of fertility and is often depicted wearing crescent amulets. A marble head of a female goddess, thought to be Aphrodite, was also found in the confines of the temple.

Inside the circular enclosure, and obviously of central importance, was a square basin built into the ground, with walls of approx. 1.5m, and of a similar depth. It was thought originally to have had a roof over it, supported by four pillars. It was the most sacred of the wells, almost certainly presided over by women, and contained the helium.

The Celts would have believed that the gentle bubbles rising to the surface of the water were the numinous essence of the deities. Helium has no specific medicinal purpose. The unique quality which most people know about is that if inhaled, it raises the pitch of the breather's voice, giving it the 'chipmunk' effect for a few seconds. People do it as an amusing sideshow when inflating party balloons. It's impossible to know whether this effect could ever have been produced by using the water from this basin in some way – or what the Celts would have thought about it, if it had. But, because the site is so atmospheric, *Les Fontaines Salées* provoke wild flights of fancy about vast underground caverns being filled with the stuff, and Celtic druids conducting their most secret offices in hidden limestone caverns – speaking in weird voices – dumbfounding their constituency with the sheer strangeness of it all…

This inner sanctuary was partially built on by the Romans when constructing their baths. It became the thermal baths exclusively for women, presided over by women, presumably out of respect for its ancient use.

Is this an echo of Geoffrey of Monmouth's 'Avalon' and what he calls in **Vita Merlini** "the court of maidens"? <u>Is it the ancient sanctuary where "nine sisters give pleasant laws to those who come from our parts to them"?</u>

The other temple was a large area, shaped like a T. It also contained a sacred basin. But this one was bigger – some 13m square – which, according to the discovery of *ex votos*, was concerned specifically with healing. There, as well as bathing, healing rituals would have taken place with the help of the little effigies, brought to the well by the afflicted. The *ex voto* would represent the ailing body part. It could be made of stone, metal or wood. From *Les Fontaines Salées* the finds include heads, hands, feet – and a pierced phallus – which is thought to have been suspended above the basin.

Although the official religion of the Roman Empire became Christianity after Emperor Constantine converted in the previous century, it would have been a long time before the old Celtic and Roman gods became obsolete. Despite the growing Christian infrastructure – and the claims of fervent and fanatical monks, Christianity was only just beginning to make an impact in Gaul at the start of the fifth century. It wasn't until the end of the century that King Clovis converted (496 AD).

By the fifth century, it is thought that the Roman baths and buildings at *Les Fontaines Salées* had probably been destroyed by barbarians – or fallen into disuse with the collapse of the Empire. But there are finds of coins and *ex-votos* which suggest that the healing wells and salt springs continued to be used for religious and commercial purposes long after the destruction of the baths.

In about the fifth century, as the Empire was collapsing, there was an extraordinarily optimistic addition to the site. At about the time Arthur Riothamus was in Burgundy, the Christian Chapel of *St. Jean-Baptiste* was built. It was optimistic because the ever-present power-struggle between the colonising Germanic tribes made nonsense of any long-term building projects. Marauding armies were filling the vacuum left by the Romans and ransacking their way through Gaul, leaving smouldering buildings and bodies in their wake. Or they might have been. There is no proof that *Les Fontaines Salées* was affected by the atrocities, so perhaps the Christians were confident that their new chapel would survive. No one knows whether there had been any marauding barbarians in that region. Neither does anyone know what happened to the pagan community of women who worshipped Diana and Venus (Aphrodite) and presided over the sanctuaries. Did they embrace the new religion before or after the time that Arthur Riothamus was in Burgundy?

The nearest place to *Les Fontaines Salées* was called *Vezeliacum*, thought to be named after a wealthy Roman who had a villa built a few kilometres away from the wells. The small, but prosperous village which grew up around *Vezeliacum* was in the shadow of a hill which was destined to become one of the most important places in medieval Christendom. By the Middle Ages the walled town, and Romanesque churches built up the sides of the steep hill and crowned with the Abbey and basilica dedicated to Mary Magdalene, was known as *Vézelay*.

But in Arthur Riothamus' time it was a wooded hill, known as the 'Scorpion' with some grazing land and grapevines scattering the south-east slope. That first settlement at the bottom of the hill is now called *St. Père-sous-Vézelay*, and *Vézelay* itself is now a UNESCO World Heritage site.

The story of *Les Fontaines Salées* and the earliest legends about the beginnings of *Vézelay*, are central to King Arthur's presence in Burgundy.

MORGEN LE FAY

Were *Les Fontaines Salées,* the healing sanctuary described by Geoffrey of Monmouth, presided over by *Morgen le Fay* of whom he says:

> "and of those sisters, she who is higher becomes a doctor in the art of healing and exceeds her sisters in excellent form. Morgen is her name, and she has learned what usefulness all the herbs bear so that she may cure sick bodies......men say that she has taught mathematics to her sisters….."?

If they were, then Arthur had two reasons for going there. Firstly to care for his – and his soldiers' wounds, and secondly to see Morgen le Fay. Legend tells us that Morgen was Arthur's older half-sister – born to Ygerne and Gorlois before Arthur's father, Uther Pendragon, married her. There is always the possibility that she was originally based on a 'real' person. There might be some evidence to link her with Avallon. For example, was she married to a local prince or king? Perhaps Morgen and the 'sisters' had been educated in medicine, music and mathematics at the famous school in

Avallon. If they existed, this community of women could have been either pagan or Christian.

Certainly, on the subject of Morgen le Fay, *Chrétien de Troyes* writing in French during the second part of the twelfth century, associates Morgen with Avalon. As previously mentioned, Avalon was a very real place for *Chrétien de Troyes*. At the wedding of Eric and Enide, in his first Arthurian Romance, he describes the 'lord' of Avalon, Guingamar, as "the friend of Morgen le Fay, and it was the proven truth."

It is also recorded that within the likely timespan that Arthur Riothamus could have been in Burgundy, there was a succession of important Burgundian kings and lords, mostly beginning with the letter G, called, *'Gundahar' 'Gundioc' 'Gundobad' 'Godomar'* and *'Godegisel'*. *Chrétien* also mentions that Morgen le Fay was King Arthur's sister, and that she was well-known for her healing powers.

At the beginning of the story of **The Knight of the Lion,** *Yvain* is discovered mad, naked and exhausted by a Lady and her maid. The Lady had, "an ointment from Morgen le Fay that could heal madness" and so she instructed her maid to use it sparingly (it was expensive) on his forehead.

Further testimony comes from a surprising source. *Giraldus Cambrensis* (Gerald of Wales, eyewitness to the discovery of the 'tomb of King Arthur & Guinevere' at Glastonbury) gives us a sober account of the 'real' Morgen:

> " ... *after Arthur had been mortally wounded there, his body was taken to the Isle of Avalon, [which is now called Glastonbury[36]], by a noble*

> *matron and kinswoman named Morgen; afterwards the remains were buried, according to her direction, in the holy burial ground."*

Given that he was writing about events that had taken place seven hundred years earlier, Gerald is no more likely to know whether Morgen was a 'noble matron' or a fully-qualified Herbalist. But he does seem to be convinced that she was 'real'.

Following the story in **Vita Merlini**, Geoffrey of Monmouth actually says two different things about Morgen's involvement in Arthur's demise. He says that Arthur was "carried over the sea with you" (Morgen). If the battle of Camblan was in England then clearly, if Glastonbury was the destination afterwards, then a sea-going vessel would not have been necessary.

In another section, however, he elaborates:

> "Thither after the battle of Camlan we took the wounded Arthur, guided by Barinthus to whom the waters and the stars of heaven were well known. With him steering the ship we arrived there with the prince, and Morgen received us with fitting honour, and in her chamber she placed the king on a golden bed ...."

This not only confirms that *Avallon* was a sea-journey away – requiring an experienced captain who could navigate by the stars, but also that Morgen didn't travel in the boat, but was there, in *Avallon*, ready and waiting to receive the wounded king in her chamber.

Once on the golden bed:

> "with her own hand she uncovered his honourable wound and gazed at it for a long time. At length she said that health could be restored to him if he stayed with her for a long time and made use of her healing art."

This description is strongly authentic as a medical examination. The hands-on, systematic examination, taking a long while, leading to the carefully considered diagnosis, is almost a text book procedure. This kind of detail could have come back to Geoffrey of Monmouth as another echo of a contemporary account. The report perhaps of one of Arthur Riothamus' soldiers who got back to Britain from *Avallon,* and whose story passed into folklore?

According to Geoffrey's account they were fully-confident in Morgen's ability and:

> "Rejoicing, therefore, we entrusted the king to her and returning spread our sails to the favouring winds."

There is one more reason why Arthur could have chosen to go to *Avallon*. Everyone knows the legend about Mordred being the love child of an incestuous relationship between Arthur and his half-sister Morgen le Fay. Trying to sort out Arthur's relatives from the legends of the Welsh, Scottish, English and Breton sources requires a brain like a memory stick. However, Arthur's central tragedy – in almost every account of his life to the present day – is that he failed to produce a legitimate heir. Such a situation would have been devastating for a king. Perhaps his catastrophic defeat in battle had given him a new urgency to find a solution. Perhaps his close call with death sent him to Morgen le Fay – the mother of his child, who knew where that child was. Could the legendary child have been based on Morvandus or Arvandus who had betrayed Arthur Riothamus' position to Euric, King of the Visigoths?

Are there any other local sites with place names that might suggest a connection? I have found a local reference which does link the name Morgen with Avallon. It's pretty obscure. I think that this is the kind of thing that the *Sociétié de Mythologie Française* might mean by 'hazy Celtic legends'.

According to Jacques Bonnet:[37]

> *"Ici le nom d'Avallon qui signifie la 'pomme', évoque un site celtique et trois pommes en triangle étaient le symbole de la déesse gauloise Rigani (qui signifie 'Reine'). La Morrigan ('Grande Reine') celtique porte le même nom de 'reine' que la petite martyre d'Alésia. Les pommes, ainsi que les baies plus petites en forme de pommes, caractérisaient des lieux enchanteurs d'où l'on pouvait passer d'un monde à l'autre ......"*

[Translation: Here, the name Avallon which means 'apple' suggests a Celtic site, and three apples together in the shape of a triangle was the symbol of a Gaul goddess called Rigani (which means

'Queen'). **The Celtic <u>La Morrigan</u> ('Great Queen'), has the same name as the queen who was the young martyr at *Alésia* (sic).** Apples, and small berries in the shape of apples, characterised enchanted places where one is able to pass between one world and the other ....]

Alésia is, of course, a very important ancient site. It's where Caesar defeated Vercingetorix. Any traveller in fifth century Gaul would know about that. While the actual story of the martyred girl, Alise Sainte Reine does not ring any Arthurian bells at all (many think her story is taken directly from another saint, Margarette of Antioch) her location within the 'magic triangles' of esoteric Celtic topography is significant. (See later: Avallon – The Poetic Landscape.) She might well have become the Christian 'replacement' saint for an actual Queen Morrigan who, in her turn, passed into legend.

Looking for fairies (French for fairy is *fée* or *fay* or variations) has always been a dubious occupation. Nevertheless, I set out to see what the area had to offer. I located a *Grotte des Fées* on the map and found it the first time I tried. Which was surprising as it was in the middle of a forest full of bluebells and wood anemones somewhere in the commune of *Brosses*. Then I failed to find it again, on three subsequent occasions. In the fifth century that would have been the fault of the cave – making itself disappear.

There are also some *'Roches des Fées'* in The *Morvan* near *Quarré-les-Tombes*. These are a curious, if natural phenomenon. If you are wont to see creatures in rock formations, read faces into patterns of lichen and imagine fissures to be gateways to the otherworld, then these are for you. But here I suffered an imagination crash. Perhaps this was to do with the iron spikes driven into the rocks at strategic places, presumably to aid climbers. It made the place utilitarian, sporty even. It had nothing of the fairies about it. But the dogs enjoyed it.

On a less heady note, perhaps Morgen le Fay had a chamber at *Les Fontaines Salées*? Someone had living accommodation there. In the official Guide Book[38], there is only one building referred to as a dwelling "*Habitat de sauniers (IVe siècle)*" [Translation: salt-merchant's house]. I suppose that's what it could be – but it could also be a priestess's or wise woman's house, for example. The only evidence left are the foundations which were covered by brambles for centuries.

Is there anything about *Les Fontaines Salées* which suggests a '*fée*' presence? Everything becomes more plausible with these few lines taken from *La Chanson de Girart de Roussillon* (see the next section)[39]:

> "*D'ire qu'en a Girarz a lo cors grin:*
> *Per tan test descenduz desoz un pin*
> *E fichat s'ensegnere laz un marbrin,*
> *Un perrun d'anti tans del **vieil elfin**,*
> *Qu'ot ja castel en l'aige, en revolin;*
> *Lodoïs li fundeit per un matin*
> *Quant le desiretet d'iquel aisin.*
> *Girarz puie el perron **le grant douvin** ...."*
>
> [Translation: Because he was angry, Girart had a heavy heart. He rode down under a pine tree on his horse. **He put down his colours on a block of**

marble – an ancient platform from antiquity – the platform of an old elfin that a long time ago had lived in a chateau in the middle of the turbulent water of the River {Cure}. Girart climbed up on this platform belonging to the great soothsayer/seer {my emphasis}...]

So the legend came down, by Geoffrey of Monmouth's time, via *'La Chanson de Girart de Roussillon'* that there had been a 'wise seer' living close by the River *Cure*, at *Les Fontaines Salées*. The 'seer' or 'soothsayer' doesn't have a name in the epic other than 'elfin'.

As a postscript to the story of the wells thus far, the extraction of salt continued intermittently until the 14th century, when the monks chose to bury the site, so that the townspeople had to use the Church's *Grenier à Sel* (salt store), and pay them the prohibitive salt tax rather than help themselves to what had always been available to them at *Les Fontaines Salées*. The wells drifted into distant memory, and then finally they were forgotten altogether. In effect, that is how they remained until *Les Fontaines Salées* were rediscovered very recently, in the twentieth century.

If Arthur Riothamus was in *Avallon* around 470 AD, beside the River *Cure* tending his wounds at *Les Fontaines Salées,* then he was on land that was highly charged with history, magic and mysticism, dedicated to bodily health, well-being and fertility. He may have been there with his sister, Morgen le Fay – perhaps herself the one-time consort of a king of Burgundy – who was treating him with herbal medicines.

What was certainly true, was that the site had been an ancient cemetery in sacred surroundings beside a sacred river. There had been a community of women there following a Romano/Celtic religion. There may have been a Christian chapel there, or that could have been later. When Arthur Riothamus was there, there was a healing basin with waters rich in minerals – still in use. There was a shrine dedicated to Diana – still in use. There were the ruins of a Roman spa. There were wells rich in salt water for washing clean the wounds of bloody battle. But above all, there was the intense spiritual power concentrated on a site which had been used since Neolithic times for healing and worship. For Arthur Riothamus it would have been the ultimate, ancestral Celtic experience.

We need to leave him there for a while – at the beginning of the Dark Ages – as we look at another story altogether, which has bearing on the authenticity of the Healing Sanctuary.

THE CHANSON DE GESTE OF GIRART DE ROUSSILLON

Chansons de Geste were part of what is known as 'The Matter of France'. They were sung troubadour stories of the military and religious heroics mainly of Charlemagne and his Paladins against the Moorish invasion. The 'Paladins', Charlemagne's crack troops of which Girart de Roussillon was a named member, can be compared with the Knights of the Round Table. Their brave exploits thrilled the courts of Medieval France. The most famous story is the **Chanson de Roland** about the Battle of *Roncevaux Pass*. They compare with 'The Matter of Britain', the legendary history of Britain and, of course, King Arthur.

Girart de Roussillon was written down at about the same time as Geoffrey of Monmouth's **History**. Although anonymous, it is thought to be based on an ancient epic poem and recorded by a monk either in *Vézelay* or *Asquins* some time between 1136 and 1180. Like all similar tales of that time it contains legendary matter spattered with fact, miraculous religious events, marvellous weapons, bloody battles and impossibly evil or saintly people who may, or may not, have actually existed. In this case, *Girart de Roussillon* and his wife *Berthe* were most definitely real. They lived in the 9th century and are credited as the founders of *Vézelay*. How much of their story is real, as told in this *Chanson de Geste*, will never be known. But, we have a medieval *Vézelay* Chronicler in *Hugues de Poitiers*, who is our main reality check. His account of the history of *Vézelay* is vivid and absorbing. Regarding the early history, it must be remembered that he is writing from a distance of 300 years. But first a brief synopsis of the legend.

The **Chanson de Girart de Roussillon** is just what you might expect a conscientious but bored monk to spend his winter months in *Asquins* writing down. It's heavy on religion and morality. It's heavy on jealousy, rivalry, hubris and treachery. It's ten thousand lines of old French, plus an epilogue – which makes it hard-going unless you're a French medievalist. But as an ancient tale about Avallon and the surrounding area which was to become Burgundy – it's like finding buried treasure.

The story begins with a rivalry between two nobles: Charles the Bald (who was also 'real' – and bald) and *Girart de Roussillon*. Charles, the King of France, controls the north of France. *Girart,* the Duke of Burgundy, controls the south

The Holy Roman Emperor of the east in Constantinople, was having the usual trouble with 'barbarians'. This time the 'barbarians' were the 'Saracens'. At the Pope's behest, both *Girart* and *Charles* went to the Emperor's aid. As a reward for their services the Emperor had promised them each one of his daughters in marriage. As the highest ranking noble, King Charles was to get *Berthe* the more senior and serious daughter, and *Girart* was to get *Elissent* – the younger of the two. By all accounts, *Elissent* was beautiful and *Berthe* was – an intelligent and saintly woman. Of course when he saw her, the King, being a shallow chauvinist, wanted *Elissent* as the trophy, instead of *Berthe* and petulantly demanded he have her. *Girart* was a loyal subject and immediately offered to swap – but not before poor *Elissent* had fallen hopelessly in love with *Girart.* She didn't much like the look of Charles who was, of course, bald. In fact, she never fell out of love with *Girart* even though her sister *Berthe* now, quite properly, occupied *Girart's* thoughts. The King was furiously jealous – not only because *Girart* was now loved by both sisters, but also because he had a sneaking suspicion that saintly *Berthe* was probably the more suited to being his Queen after all, and he'd made the wrong choice.

Charles took out his anger on *Girart* by capturing *Girart's* castle near *Châtillon-sur-Seine*, thus beginning a series of wars and counter-wars. *Girart* retreated to *Avallon* and gathered around him a very large army. His father, '*Drogon',* and his uncle were brought into the fray. As was the custom in those days, a battle was 'arranged' between the two sides. Like a contest, there was a date, place and time agreed where the two conflicting sides would make combat. The winner would be compensated. The battle was to take place beside the River *Cure* at *'Vaubeton'* – which is of course, right by the site of *Les Fontaines Salées.*

The Battle of *Vaubeton* began on a beautiful May morning:

Mult par sunt gent li plan de Vaubetun
Granz catre leges durent en un randun.
N'I a maupaz ne feign, bos ne gasun,
Mai spur l'aige d'Arsanz per devisun.
Carles Martels chevauge a Avalun;
Cuidet le castrel prendre, mais riend non fun.
Per tant s'en vait Folchers vers Roussilun,
[E] encontret Draugon e Widelun ......
Devers l'un cao s'en intrent dinz Vaubetun.
Aiqui verraz drecar tant gonfanun,
Tant ensegnes de gisez e tan penun,
Mais de set leges firent de porpreisun.
Ce diraz, ses vissaz per plan cambun,
Conques puis en is secle tau genz ne fun.

> [Translation: The plains of Vaubeton are so beautiful! They stretch for four leagues in one piece without a bad way of crossing, with no marshes, no woods, no undergrowth. Only the river Arsen {River Cure} cuts across them. Charles Martel (sic) rides towards Avallon: he intended to take the castle, but he could do nothing. ... So Fourchier made off towards Roussillon and met up with Drogon and

85

Odilon ... as they were just emerging on to the plain of Vaubeton. Oh what banners, what many-coloured standards and flags in the space of these seven leagues! Had you but seen them on this open plain you would have said that there had never been such an assembly on this earth.]

The 'open plain' beside the River *Cure* stretches from *Les Fontaines Salées* to the *Champ de Bataille* at *Sermizelles/Givry*, at the confluence of the *Cousin* and *Cure*. It was the site of the famous *Vaudonjon* necropolis (see page 152), and of a large fifth century agricultural community.[40]

The battle was fiercely fought between evenly-matched soldiers. It raged from dawn to dusk and the River *Cure* ran with the blood of the dead. It was lamented by the troubadours that:
> "*cent mille dames sont veuves de leurs maris.*"
> [Translation: A hundred thousand ladies were widowed that day.]

Drogon, named as *Girart's* father, was killed, after demonstrating his bravery by riding up and down in front of the troops, taunting the enemy. The fighting came to a sudden end when a violent thunderstorm swept through the valley. Lightning bolts struck the battle colours flying on the ends of the soldiers' lances. Both sides were affected and agreed to finish the fighting because they saw it as divine intervention. The soldier who had killed *Drogon* was exiled as compensation for *Girart*, and an uneasy peace with *Charles* was sustained for a few years.

To cut a long story short, many more battles between the two eventually ensued. *Girart* and *Berthe* became paupers living in the forest as charcoal-burners. After many years *Elissent* interceded on their behalf with her husband and they were given back their chateau in *Roussillon* and their lands around *Avallon*.

The last episode of the story has *Girart* and *Berthe* founding the first religious community in what is now *St.-Père-sous-Vézelay* (*Les Fontaines Salées*).

The biggest surprise of all though, and an astonishing revelation given the times, is that the first monastery founded by *Girart de Roussillon* and his wife *Berthe*, was a **monastery for women**.

The 'official' history of *Vézelay* is recorded in a Chronicle written between 1140 – 1160 AD. This confirms that the first Abbey was founded by *Girart de Roussillon* in the original location of
> '*Vézelay* in the valley of the River *Cure*, on or near what is now *St. Père-sous-Vézelay*'.

In fact, *Girart* and his wife *Berthe* founded two monasteries, one in *Pothières* near *Châtillon-sur-Seine*, and the one at *Vézelay*.

This is confirmed in a Charter signed by *Girart* and dated 850 AD, as recorded by *Hugues de Poitiers*:

> "In similar fashion we have founded ... another monastery, as a dwelling for handmaidens of God living under the strict rule and institutes of the blessed St. Benedict, in the place or land called

Vézelay, in the county of Avallon, in the kingdom of Burgundy..."[41]

But there was something strange about this monastery for 'handmaidens', right from the start. It was endowed generously, and had built-in protection provided by the pope himself. The nuns were also able to elect their own Abbess. All these privileges were embedded in the Charter. It should have thrived as a community – but it didn't. In an essay by E.L.Cox some more interesting facts are revealed:

> "Not a single document has survived to indicate who the original sisters were or how many of them there were, nor is there any documentation at all that bears witness to the activities of a functioning community. There is no mention of any Abbess of Vézelay, which has led to speculation that perhaps there never was one other than Countess Berthe or her daughter Eva who are thought to have associated themselves with the community at some point."[42]

How mysterious in the first place to found a women's community – which would have been a rarity as a first consideration at that time. But then, how extraordinary to have no records of its existence at all. After *Berthe* and *Girart* died, there is no further reference to the monastery by the River *Cure* except:

> "...on 19 September 877 Pope John VIII, then on his way to France for the Council of Troyes, gave his approval for the conversion of the abbey into a house for men."[43]

So, for whatever reason, it failed as a female community and was replaced by a monastery for men. Later it was moved to the top of the *Vézelay* hill – the reason always given being greater safety from the attentions of 'barbarians'. By this time, the 'barbarians' were Norse invaders who came up the River *Seine* to Paris – and were 'given' Burgundy to pillage as compensation, if they left Paris alone. Consequently, they continued their journey up the *River Yonne* and destroyed the abbey of *Saint-Rémy-de-Vareilles* near *Sens,* and burned the abbey of *Saint-Germain* in *Auxerre*. They then divided into two flanks – one proceeding up the *River Armançon* to seize *Flavigny* some sixty kilometres to the east of *Vézelay*. Legend has it that the second flank took the *River Cure* "in the first month of the year 887" [44]and destroyed the hamlet and monastery. These were the events which caused a new, fortified abbey to be constructed at the top of the hill. And, of course, this heralded the start of the dramatic rise of *Vézelay*.

Vézelay became a shrine to *Mary Magdalene*. *Vézelay* became a pilgrimage centre on the way to *Compostella*. *Vézelay* became the celebrated departure point of Richard the Lionheart's Crusade to the Holy Land.

If the account of the Norsemen coming up the River *Cure* is true then it proves one thing, at least. It proves that there was a navigable waterway from the English Channel via the rivers *Seine, Yonne* and *Cure* to *Les Fontaines Salées*. But unlike the atrocities committed at *Sens*, *Auxerre* and *Flavigny*, there is no hard evidence to suggest that Vikings or any other 'barbarians' reached the little monastery beside the River *Cure*.

So, what can we make of all that in terms of the story of Arthur in France? We left him at *Les Fontaines Salées*, about to disappear into the tunnel of the Dark Ages. With the

Chanson de Girart de Roussillon we rejoin the story of *Les Fontaines Salées* 400 years later.

At both ends of the 'tunnel', in legend and in fact, we find a community of women. In the fifth century they were the healing guardians of Diana's sanctuary. In the 9th century the first thing we discover is a Christian nunnery on the selfsame spot. What happened to that community throughout the Dark Ages? Did it survive in a different form to provide a link back to Arthurian times in Gaul?

We can only speculate. Perhaps the women maintained their pagan authority to begin with, which then became an enduring problem for the new Christian religion. The Christian church may have replicated the behaviour of the Romans with the Druids, disbanded the women, removed them from their sacred shrine, and replaced them with men. They could have covered up the evidence with layers of new belief, miracles, a bewildering number of 'saints' and a new building. Was a plausible story woven for posterity to explain why the community failed?

The blame, as ever, falls on the 'barbarians'. It may well be true that all tangible evidence of a pagan religion can be destroyed: the pagan shrines – the buildings – the altars – the wooded glades – the icons – the temples – the effigies. But the one element that can't be destroyed is water: the sacred streams and wells. They can be filled in – buried – as they eventually were at *Les Fontaines Salées* – but they will always find a way of reappearing. Water will continue in its cycle despite man's best efforts.

REDISCOVERING *LES FONTAINES SALÉES*

The story of the rediscovery of *Les Fontaines Salées* is curious. It is fiction made fact – the result of following a legend to its source, and finding elements of the truth, but also finding further mystery. Not until comparatively recent times was the full story revealed.

In 1891 a medievalist, *Paul Meyer*, encouraged his promising student, *Léon Mirot* to do some field work and verify topography in *Girart de Roussillon* – particularly in relation to the area around *Vézelay*. With his *Chanson de Geste* under his arm, *Léon* set out to find the site of the 'Battle of Vaubeton'. He identified a small valley near *Foissy-le-Vézelay* called *Vaux Bertin* or *Vau Bouton*, which fitted the description and location in the text. Some forty years later *Léon* returned with a young man called *René Louis*, who wanted to find out why the troubadours – originators of the *Chanson* – had chosen a real location for what was considered to be a legendary battle.

Between 1930 and 1933 they conducted some more research together – finding further topographical evidence, and also local knowledge of an ancient battle that had, in fact, taken place close to the *River Cure*. In 1934 René set off to walk the overgrown fields by the river. In particular he wanted to have a look at the place where the troubadours sang of a ruined chateau once belonging to *Elfin*, of which a large piece of rock and the foundations of the castle towers were still visible. What he discovered hidden in the undergrowth, of course, were not the foundations of a castle, but the circular foundations of the Celtic temple, the salt wells, and the ruins of the Gallo-Roman baths. Since 1935 the site has been the subject of archaeological research by the state, and has been classified as an Historic Monument.

An exciting example of legend-made-fact. Nowadays the site itself is presented very modestly. One of its charms is that the wells and foundations are simply there – in open, tranquil fields beside the River *Cure*. You can pump up some salty water and taste it – watch the lazy bubbles of helium drift to the surface. You can wander around the remains of hot, cold and tepid Roman baths and their heating systems. You can listen to the wind whisper through the aspens. If you look up to the north-west it's now possible to see the *Vézelay* basilica, although in Arthur's time *Vézelay* was no more than a strange, scorpion-shaped hill. Above all, you can take the time to sense the super-charged landscape that has been there since the dawn of time. There is nothing to inhibit your enjoyment, or imagination. No fences – no jobsworths. The result is a site which maintains its integrity and hasn't yet fallen prey to touristification. This is one of those sites which exceeds all expectation. The tiny museum in *St. Père-sous-Vézelay* houses the archaeological finds. It is like walking into someone's front room – but don't let that detract you from appreciating the worldwide significance of the material.

5
AVALLON – THE FORGES

DROGON & PENDRAGON

We haven't quite finished with the **Chanson de Girart de Roussillon**. In particular, we haven't finished with '*Drogon*', *Girart's* 'father'.

The name '*Drogon*' and its derivations are not to be treated lightly. It is a name full of mythic potential. *Drogon* was killed during the Battle of Vaubeton. He was killed despite the fact that he was wearing:

> "*un haubert merveilleux sorti de la forge d'Espandragon; jamais armes n'avaient pu le trouer.*"
> [Translation: a marvellous coat of mail made in the forge of Pendragon, which had never been penetrated by any weapon.]

The footnote in the French edition cites Paul Meyer as making a positive connection between the name of the forge and the name 'Pendragon' associated with King Arthur's father.[45]

In the 12th century it was common practice for royalty and noblemen to have their own dedicated teams of smiths or 'forgerons' to supply their weapons and armoury. A '*haubert*' was a flexible chain mail tunic made of small metal pieces riveted together. It had vents front and back to facilitate horse-riding. There was usually a monk-like hood attached which protected the head and neck.[46] What is *Drogon* doing wearing this special armour with invincible properties? This is where two different literary cycles collide. Suddenly we have The Matter of France directly cross-referenced with The Matter of England. Suddenly we have the juxtaposition of a place, a name and a battle with the first Dragon King, Arthur's father. And here we are, in the middle of Avallon, Burgundy.

So who was *Drogon*? Not *Girart de Roussillon's* flesh and blood father, that's for sure, not with a name like that. His 'real' father was apparently *Leuthard Ist*, Count of *Frézensac* from the Pyrenees region[47]. In the **Chanson**, *Drogon* was a bold, fearless old warrior, a nobleman unafraid to take on the whole of Charles' army single-handed if needs be. In short, he is a chip off the old block – an echo of the Dragon King himself. If we trace his progress through the **Chanson** up until his death then we find even more resonances.

In the words of a footnote to the *Lettres gothiques* [48]edition, *Drogon* first appears rather 'abruptly' in the *Chanson*. He is given a special mention amongst the most noble delegates at the court of King Charles in Reims at Pentecost, and in the presence of the archbishop. You had to be a 'grand seigneur' even to be invited, and *Drogon* is named as being there with ten of his vassals. He is actually referred to as 'a sage' when he begins to tell the story of the Emperor and his two daughters – fulfilling his essential role in the narrative of the *Chanson*. But what is most curious, is that he addresses the distinguished gathering **in his own**

tongue ..."*Le sage Drogon prit la parole dans sa langue.*" If he did not speak the same language as his peers, then what language did he speak? Again a footnote suggests that it is quite common for characters throughout the *Chansons de Geste* to speak foreign languages, but that the convention is, that everyone understands them anyway – for the sake of the story ... But *Drogon* is supposed to be Burgundian – his son is a Count of Burgundy. Could this be an indication that *Girart's* ancestry did not, in fact, come from Burgundy? Or has *Drogon* the character been 'borrowed' from somewhere else entirely?

When he is next mentioned, *Drogon* is going off on behalf of the Empire to fight against the Spanish pagans with his brother *Odilon* and their joint armies – an activity for which he is renowned throughout the civilised world. This is very similar to the actions of Arthur Riothamus and his army when he came to Gaul to fight the Visigoths from Spain.

The inevitable build-up to the Battle of Vaubeton has Girart calling on his father's help to win back his lands from King Charles. *Drogon* returns from Spain and responds to the call to arms and dresses himself for the battle due to take place beside the *River Cure* in the *Avallonnais*:

"As vos per mi l'estor le viel Draugon,
Le paired an Girart, l'oncle Folcon.
E sist el cheval bai godemucon,
E vesti son auberc merevillon
Qu'issi de la fornaise Espandragon;
Oncques enquer par armes falsaz ne fon,
E a lacat son elme de baraton;
L'orbre ab aur e a peires tot d'envoron

*Plus resplent que Estelle ki luis el tron
E a ceinte l'espade de Marmion;
Escut portet e lance a gonfanon."*[49]

> [Translation: Here amongst the mêlée is old Drogon, father to Girart and uncle to Fouque. He sat astride a bay horse from Ghadames and **was cloaked in a marvellous chain mail from Pendragon's forge: no arms could penetrate it.** He laced up his ceremonial helmet whose gold and precious stones shone more brightly than a star in the heavens. At his waist was Marmion's sword and he bore a shield and a bannered lance.]

Here is a passage from Geoffrey of Monmouth's *History*. King Arthur is dressing himself for the battle of Bath:

> "Arthur himself put on a leather jerkin worthy of so great a king. On his head he placed a golden helmet, with a crest carved in the shape of a dragon; and across his shoulders a circular shield called Pridwen, on which there was painted a likeness of the Blessed Mary, Mother of God, which forced him to be thinking perpetually of her. **He girded on his peerless sword, called Caliburn, which was forged in the Isle of Avalon.** A spear called Ron graced his right hand: long, broad in the blade and thirsty for slaughter."[50]

In a passage that is surely too similar to be purely coincidence, this is the only time when Geoffrey describes Arthur's battle dress – but most importantly, **it is also the only other time that he mentions 'Avalon' in his *History*, and he too talks about a forge in connection with Arthur's famous sword, 'Caliburn'.**

The Oxford manuscript of the **Chanson de Girart** was written in an intermediate language between 'langue d'oc' and 'langue d'oïl' sometime between 1136 and 1180 and thought to have been copied by two different people either in northern Italy or Provence. Geoffrey's **History** was written in Latin, probably in Oxford, England sometime between 1129 and 1151. Given those dates, the different languages of the texts, and the distances involved, it seems most likely that if there were a connection beyond coincidence between these two passages, then either the anonymous author of the **Chanson** took a leaf out of Geoffrey's book, or that they were both independently in possession of earlier source material linking the Pendragon dynasty with Burgundy, and *Avallon*.

Uther Pendragon, Arthur's father, was the first 'Dragon' king. In brief, this is what Geoffrey of Monmouth says about him:

"... the King [Constantine] had three sons .... Their names were Constans, Aurelius and Utherpendragon."[51]

As a boy he is sent to *Armorica* (Brittany) with his brother Aurelius to be brought up in safety away from the machinations of Vortigern. The question is, did Uther Pendragon ever travel from Brittany to *Avallon*? Perhaps he came more than once, and gave his name to a forge that produced his own weapons and armour of the highest quality. I'm certain that enterprising 'forgerons' were not above identifying their businesses with important and well-known people with local connections even then, in much the same way as there are countless tea rooms 'belonging' to 'Arthur' or 'Pendragon' the length and breadth of the west country in England today. However if this were to be the case, then there is still the question which needs to be answered. What is the link between the Pendragon dynasty and Avallon?

Geoffrey goes on with the tale. When they are old enough, Aurelius and Uther Pendragon return to fight for their birthright, against Vortigern and the Saxons. Aurelius eventually becomes king but is poisoned.

At this time the brilliant comet appears in the sky (442 AD?) as previously mentioned. The tail of the comet was in the shape of a dragon. Merlin's interpretation:

> **"The star signifies you in person, and so does the fiery dragon beneath the star"**

led to Uther Pendragon fighting for the throne of Britain as the only surviving brother.[52]

When he became king, Uther Pendragon had two dragons crafted in gold. One he gave to Winchester, and the other he kept to carry around with him in war, as a talisman.

> "From that moment onwards he was called Utherpendragon, which in the British language means 'a dragon's head'."[53]

The dragon was Pendragon's symbol, the emblem of his kingship which was passed on to Arthur, who, as indicated above, wore the image of a dragon on his helmet. And what of Merlin's prophecy about the extent of Arthur's realm? Prophesies are easy in hindsight – a gift to someone like Geoffrey of Monmouth. There will never be an answer of course, but it is precisely these 'echoes' of distant legends that provide us with clues – tiny fragments that may help us create a larger picture of King Arthur in France.

So is this *'Drogon'* in the *Chanson de Girart de Roussillon* a memory of another powerful old warrior who died in the saddle? In the legend, could he have been a direct descendant of Uther Pendragon? In reality, could he have been a reference to Arthur Riothamus himself who stayed on in *Avallon* after his wounds were cured, fought again with the Burgundians and was eventually killed on a battlefield beside the River *Cure*? In either case, how did *Drogon* come into possession of his marvellous *'haubert'*? Was he given it, or did he simply do his shopping at the same forge?

Did *Drogon's* coat of mail have the same provenance as Arthur's sword, Caliburn? Was there a superior forge in the Avallonnais area with a reputation for producing miraculously strong weapons and armour?

THE FORGES

The answer is yes, probably. In fact there were a great many forges in the *Avallonnais* area dating back to Celtic times.

The Celts are remembered for their mining and metal-working skills and their imaginative and creative ingenuity. This not only gave them a practical edge on other civilisations when it came to weaponry, shields, tools and agricultural implements, but also established them as the western world's creative artists and craftsmen. They excelled at jewellery-making, fine art and precious metalcraft. This industry became the basis of their foreign trade and wealth-generation.

It was the Celts who first discovered and exploited the iron ore deposits in the vast forests to the south-west of the *Vézelay* hill – *Les forêts des Ferrières*. The forest was delineated by several important towns now called, *Bois-de-la-Madeleine, Chamoux, Maison-Dieu, Nuars, Foissy-lès-Vézelay and Fontenay-près-Vézelay*. The Celts established the area as a major metal-working centre, with good road and water communications, which the Romans further developed and exploited, providing a network of substantial roads fit for haulage, and a navigable waterway up the River *Cure* from the River *Yonne*, as far as *Gué Pavé* which was thought to have been both a fording point, and a landing stage.

Over an area in excess of 20 square kilometres, slag heaps have been discovered, providing evidence of the smelting processes. Almost two thousand mines were discovered across an area of six hectares, and it was estimated by Abbot Lacroix in his *"Les Origines protohistoriques et gallo-romaines de Vézelay"* that between five hundred and eight hundred manual workers would have been employed in the iron industry.[54] The whole area is also dotted with the remains of forges, where the iron was processed, and with weaponry such as lances, swords and scabbards, daggers, and scramasaxes.[55] The Romans were quick to recognise the importance of the land around Avallon with its salt and mineral deposits.

There is an alternative suggestion as to the derivation of the name *Vézelay*. Rather than being named after a wealthy

Roman who had a villa built near to *Les Fontaines Salées*, some suggest that it was named after the Celtic god of forges, *Sucellus*. He was always depicted with a mallet or hammer. The Gallic prefix '*Ver*' is a superlative and means 'greatest'. The name '*Ver Sucellus*' would therefore mean the *'greatest forgeron'*.

It is impossible to know whether any one of the many forges in the area was better than any other. There are no toponymical clues either. Many place names have been Christianised and their originals largely lost. It would have been too much to ask to find a forge named 'Espandragon' – or anything remotely resembling it. We shall just have to be content with the knowledge that the iron industry was once the most significant and important activity in the whole of the *Avallonnais* region.

There is, however, a lateral connection which is fascinating to explore. An analysis of the archaeological finds discovered in the woods to the west of the *Vézelay* hill and in the River *Cure* valley, reveals that there was one vast centre of production more sizeable than all the rest – that centre was *Fontanae in pago Avalense* or *Fontenay-près-Vézelay* as it is now known. The site of *Crot-au-Port* within the commune was so pitted with mines, channels and ditches for washing the minerals that it became known as "*le trou au Cochon*" [pig hole]. Anyone who has seen what a vigorous family of wild boar can do with their snouts to a field overnight, will understand the nickname. [56]

The mining industry became regularised in the second century AD under Hadrian. The foundations of a villa dating from the third century were discovered in the middle of the

Fontanae zone. It was thought to be the dwelling of a Roman mining supervisor. There was also a 'fanum' or temple where a bronze statuette of the god Mercury was discovered. The foundations are still to be seen in the middle of the forest. Both of these buildings were on a junction between two significant roads. The first road led from the temple to *Les Fontaines Salées*, and the second road crossed the massive forests and linked *Brèves* with *St. Père sous Vézelay* and on to the little village of *Sermizelles* to join the *Via Agrippa*. (See map) This means that there were direct routes from *Sermizelles* to *Les Fontaines Salées,* and from *Sermizelles* to the vast metal-working centre of the Avallonnais.

THE SARMATIANS

The village of *Sermizelles* is on the *Via Agrippa* to the north of *Avallon*. It is at the confluence of the two rivers – the *Cousin* and the *Cure*. It is therefore at the conjunction of two important valleys – one leading to *Avallon* itself, and the other to *Les Fontaines Salées* and onwards towards *Brèves* and the west, into the *Loire* and the heart of Gaul. It is surrounded to the north and west by high chalk escarpments – and to the south and east by the granite foothills of the *Morvan*. In particular, *Montmarte* is a perfectly shaped high hill overlooking *Avallon*. There was a magnificent Roman temple discovered at the top, dedicated to the god of war, Mars. Four statues of Mars, together with numerous other finds were discovered there. There is a theory that the topography of the area more nearly fits that described by the eyewitnesses of the siege of *Alésia* – the final battle of the Gauls against Julius Caesar led by Vercingetorix.

The vast water meadows where the rivers meet is today called *Champ de Bataille* – so something occurred there. These broad, flat fields stretch almost as far as *Les Fontaines Salées*. Bronze age finds, collectively known as '*The Sermizelles Hoard*' were discovered there together with an ancient circular enclosure revealed by aerial photography and numerous sarcophaguses of the Gallo Roman era and later[57]. Local knowledge says that any band of marauding barbarians had a passing go at *Sermizelles* because of its important location. In other words, the '*Bataille*' referred to could have been any old battle. The *Champ de Bataille* would have been like the local stadium. If there was a battle to be had – it would have been held there. In the Middle Ages matters got so bad that they built a wall around the village – the remnants of which can still be seen. But the whole point about *Sermizelles* is its name.

The name *Sermizelles* is thought to come from the '*Sarmates*' or *Sarmatians* who were conscripted Roman soldiers from the near East – a region roughly corresponding to Persia.

> "*Sarmisoliae en 1199. Ce toponyme rappelle peut-être la présence d'auxiliaires Sarmates, signalés dans la Notitia Dignitatum, contrôlant la confluence Cousin-Cure et la Voie d'Agrippa: V. Petit, 1870. L'église est implantée au croisement des deux plus importantes voies antiques du sud de l'Yonne.*"[58]

[Translation: Sarmisoliae in 1199. The name recalls perhaps the presence of Sarmations, auxiliary Roman troops stationed there to control the confluence of the (rivers) *Cure* and *Cousin,* and the *Via Agrippa*: V. Petit 1870. The church is positioned

>at a crossroads of two of the most important ancient roads of the southern Yonne]

The Sarmations were an early, horse-centred nomadic civilisation. They were known to have been garrisoned as part of the Roman legion at *Camp Cora*, a few kilometres away.

Camp Cora is another one of those sites which exceeds expectation. High on the cliffs above *St. Moré*, Agrippa's road from *Boulogne* to *Lyon* swoops down over the escarpment to ford the River *Cure*. But before it does, there's a Roman spur road linking it to *Camp Cora*. Many of the very best ancient places in Burgundy are so impressive because they haven't been tampered with, in the name of tourism. To get to the *Camp* you walk down a track through the woods. You turn a corner at the end, and there rising above you are the fortifications. You can see quite clearly the ramparts built of stone in a herringbone design, and every so often there are the foundations of circular watchtowers. When I visited *Montfault* – the one that nobody believes is a fortified oppidum (see next chapter) – I was struck by the similarities of scale and dimension, and the obvious defensive purpose of the structure. There are discreet signposts telling you little pieces of information about the Via Agrippa and the construction of the *Camp* and what has been discovered there. If you go up beyond the fortifications, there is a magnificent view of the River *Cure* valley down towards *Voutenay-sur-Cure*. Up there amongst the rare wild flowers you can pick up white stones with little shell fossils in them.

But to get back to the Sarmatians. Mithraism was a popular religion amongst soldiers from the east. A small white stone head of Mithras was discovered at *Camp Cora* together with a quantity of money and ceramics which date the building of the walls and towers to the fifth century.[59]

These cavalrymen had a religious mythology strikingly similar to elements of later Arthurian romance. They had a particular reverence for swords and weaponry and maintained religious customs associating swords with stone and water. They also used the dragon emblem as their war standard.

In his book, 'Arthur the Dragon King'[60], Howard Reid presents an account of the central Asian diaspora from about 1000 BC, tracking the nomadic tribes as they galloped towards the west on their thoroughbred horses from the steppes of Russia and beyond. He tells us the names of the different waves of 'barbarians' – the Scythians, the Sarmatians, Attila and his Huns, and the Alans who were ethnically related to the Sarmatians. In his book he ends up with the theory that King Arthur was part of the Alanic tradition, and in fact that Arthur himself was based on 'King Eothar'. But for our purposes, the most interesting and feasible aspect of his theory is that, according to Howard Reid the Sarmatians invented flexible chain mail, the stirrup and used the long 'slashing' sword as opposed to the short, Scythian sword.

He celebrates the skills of the Sarmatians as riders and warriors who could shoot their arrows from horseback. He tells us about their wondrous works of art in metal, and above all he introduces us to their formidable culture which venerated their big swords and the ferocity with which they used them to sever heads and cleave bodies ... They so impressed the Romans with their weaponry and battle tactics that the Romans recruited them and deployed them in their legions the length and breadth of the Empire.

Howard Reid suggests that these tribes, rather than the indigenous Celts, had a greater influence on the subsequent legends and stories of King Arthur. He homes in on the Sarmatians who were known as 'the lizard people' – another reference to dragons. They used the dragon as a flying battle standard and there is a famous French illustrated manuscript dating from 1290 AD that shows King Arthur fighting beneath something similar[61]. Robert de Boron's "L'Estoir de Merlin" was the text for this illustration. He, of course, was a Burgundian, and the first to write about the Arthurian 'sword in the stone' episode.

It is impossible to know who influenced whom. The Celts were never one homogeneous people. They had no common language. Tribes inter-bred, or wiped each other out, creating a bewildering melting pot of ethnicity. At the same time as the Sarmatians were making inroads into the west, so the Celts were part of the drift which spread their civilisation to the north and to Britain, and to the east, west, and south of Gaul.

The central preoccupations of both Celts and Sarmatians are remarkably similar. The cult of the horse, for example, which Howard Reid admits was a Celtic virtue, he confines to the Iberian Celts. However, the Celtic horse goddess Epona was worshipped widely throughout Gaul in general. In particular, Epona had a strong following amongst soldiers and there are shrines and wells dedicated to her all over Burgundy. It was said that when Vercingetorix knew that he would be defeated by Caesar at *Alésia*, he sent the horses away as he could not bear to see them suffer.

They shared their advanced metal working skills and their fondness for the slashing sword – but the Celts had certain abilities in this area that nomadic tribes would never have possessed – their mining and smelting skills. These depended on remaining in one place. These were the skills that had been perfected by generations of workers who had stayed put and knew their land and their rocks. What is interesting though, is that it raises the exciting question, what kinds of weaponry could be produced by a society highly skilled in all aspects of mining and metalwork? What happens when you unite a race of sword-worshipping, stirrup-using cavalry warriors, protected by their flexible chain mail, with a warlike race who were the western world's finest craftsmen, mining engineers and smelters? What happens when you provide them with the means of production in an area which had been celebrated for its metal-working for over five centuries?

So, we have a place name, a date and archaeological evidence putting the Sarmations, their skills, customs and religion in *Avallon* at exactly the time when Arthur Riothamus was making his escape from *Bourges*. We have the evidence of what we know about the similarities between Celtic and Sarmatian culture. We have Geoffrey of Monmouth referring to Caliburn having been forged in 'Avalon', and we have a forge down the road capable of making *Drogon's* high quality flexible chain mail. **But above all, we have (as they say in crime circles) the opportunity.**

But this is not the end of the story. Six hundred years later we discover that Caliburn is in *Avallon* again. It may never have left. We know this because Richard the Lionheart had it in 1190 AD when he joined his greatest friend and ally, King Philippe II of France for the Third Crusade. The Crusade began at *Vézelay* which had, by then, acquired its celebrated name and reached the height of its religious fame and fortune.

CALIBURN

Geoffrey of Monmouth names the sword, Caliburn, as Arthur's weapon on three occasions. Only one of them, the 'Battle of Bath' (the earliest according to Geoffrey's chronology) is on English soil. The other two are in France: once when he delivered the death-blow to '*Frollo*' in Paris, and finally, when Arthur defeats the Romans in the heart of Burgundy, near Autun.

We are left in no doubt that Caliburn is a long 'slashing sword':

> [Battle of Bath] "He drew his sword Caliburn …. And rushed forward at full speed into the thickest ranks of the enemy. Every man whom he struck … he killed at a single blow. He did not slaken his onslaught until he had dispatched four hundred and seventy men with his sword Caliburn."

> [Fighting *Frollo*] "He raised Caliburn in the air with all his strength and brought it down through Frollo's helmet and so on to his head, which he cut in two halves. At this blow, Frollo fell to the ground,

drummed the earth with his heels and breathed his soul into the winds."

[Fighting the Romans at Autun] "He moved up with his own division, drew his wonderful sword Caliburn, and encouraged his fellow-soldiers by shouting loudly at them... Arthur dashed straight at the enemy. He flung them to the ground and cut them to pieces. Whoever came his way was either killed himself or had his horse killed under him at a single blow... Their armour offered them no protection capable of preventing Caliburn, when wielded in the right hand of this mighty King, from forcing them to vomit forth their souls with their life-blood."[62]

Geoffrey gives us no more information about what happened to Caliburn. Stories of ladies in lakes, deathbed commands and disobedient knights were to be added to the legend much later. Later even than when Richard the Lionheart went to *Vézelay* for the Third Crusade in 1190 AD. The fact that Richard had the sword, would not have conflicted with Arthur's biography as it was then known. Caliburn had not been cast into any lake by then, so it was feasible that someone, somewhere had looked after the celebrated sword for posterity.

By the time of the Crusade Arthur's 'grave' hadn't quite been 'discovered' in Glastonbury. So who had it? Where did King Richard get Caliburn from?

We know that King Richard had the sword with him at *Vézelay* as it is recorded in *Walter of Coventry's* "The

Historical Collections of Walter of Coventry" (late 13th C.) that it was given by him as a gift to King Tancred of Sicily:

> "On the fourth day, the king of Sicily sent many great gifts in both gold and silver, as well as horses and silk garments, to the English king; but he received nothing in return except a little ring, which he accepted as a token of mutual friendship. **Moreover, the king of England gave to King Tancred an excellent sword called Caliburn, formerly belonging to King Arthur of England."**

We know what a grand and splendid occasion the beginning of that third Crusade was. Not one, but two great kings descended on the area around *Avallon* and *Vézelay* with their entourages. There was almost a long-term love-affair occurring between King Richard the Lionheart and King *Philippe Auguste* of France. They were hardly out of each other's company. Before his death in 1189 Richard's father, King Henry II of England, tried many times in vain to recall Richard from King Philippe's court in France:

> "[Richard] remained with the King of France against his father's will. The King of France so honoured him that every day they dined at one table and from the one pot, and at night a bed did not separate them. And because of the strong love that seemed to be between them, the King of England, seized with great bewilderment, wondered what was going on, and being wary for himself in the future, frequently sent messengers to France to recall his son Richard"[63]

In the early days of July all the routes that led to *Vézelay* were jam-packed with mounted Crusaders with their coloured pennants, harnesses and shining weaponry. There were encampments all along the meadows beside the River *Cure,* and houses and barns in the surrounding villages were requisitioned. Only the kings and their households were accommodated in the town itself – either in the monastery or in one of the grand houses on the hill.

There is a Crusader's eyewitness account of reaching *Vézelay:*

"*Nous avons commencé le saint voyage en traversant la Bourgogne. Là dans une region où nous rencontrâmes pour la première fois des hauteurs rocheuses et escarpées, au-dessus de la rivière Cure, dominant un rocher assiégé par les vignobles verdoyants, la ville forte de Vézelay invite à bravir ses pentes par le charme de son site et l'abondance de ce jus qui réjouit les coeurs.*"[64]

[Translation: We began the sacred journey by crossing Burgundy. There, in a region where we met for the first time rocky heights and escarpments, above the River *Cure*, astride a rock surrounded by verdant grapevines, the stronghold of *Vézelay* invites one to climb its slopes by the very charm of its location and by the abundance of that juice which causes the heart to rejoice.]

After the days of ceremonies and prayer (and probably large quantities of the 'juice') the armies set off for the Holy Land; *Philippe* heading for the port of Gênes, and Richard heading for Marseille – and thence to Sicily and King Tancred.

We shall probably never know how Richard came into possession of Caliburn on that occasion. But there are really only two alternatives. He either brought it with him from England after his (very brief) visit there to raise funds for the Crusade (in which case where did he get it from?), or he was given it when he reached *Vézelay*.

My opinion is that Caliburn was buried with Arthur in *Avallon,* and at some stage – possibly when the body was disturbed – was taken from the sarcophagus and held secure throughout the intervening time, passing eventually into the hands of the Abbey at *Vézelay*. That it was presented by the Abbot to *King Philippe* on the occasion of the Third Crusade, who, then presented it to Richard the Lionheart at the start of the Crusade, that day in *Vézelay,* as a token of his love and loyalty.

But who would keep a sword and a body safe and secure for such a very long time? And where?

6
AVALLON – THE POETIC LANDSCAPE

"We come here to listen to the wind which carries us away into the world of Legend"[65]

THE MYSTICAL LANDSCAPE

'Avallonnais', the region around *Avallon* in Burgundy, has an intensely powerful atmosphere, and like Glastonbury, attracts the imaginations of those drawn by spiritual matters. Across the years, the surrounding landscape, fashioned and nourished by the gentle, bubbling waters of the River *Cure* and the River *Cousin*, has been a source of inspiration.

The area of *Avallonnais* is mystical, fertile and beautiful. Is it good enough to become part of the mainstream Arthurian legend?

Much-respected man of letters and novelist *Jules Roy* (1907 – 2000) in his book **'Vézelay – A Sentimental Guide'** thought so. He said that the route to *Vézelay*, lined with hillocks, reminded him of "King Arthur's quest for the Holy Grail." Why? A Frenchman could have chosen from a thousand home-grown literary metaphors to describe his particular bit of *la belle France*. But he chose instead a great British myth of immense potency. For *Jules Roy* it was not simply the beauty of the countryside. For him the landscape itself seemed to emit a sensual inspiration, creating a

Christian rapture, a poet's passion for the Divine, and his almost personal, spiritual love for Mary Magdalene. He is buried in the cemetery at *Vézelay*.

The area attracts artists and poets. Nobel prize-winner, *Romain Rolland* (1866-1944), was brought up in Avallonnais:

> "... (in) the sky-blue flax and the water of her rivers I found, in my childhood, all the footprints of the universe."

He eventually lived in *Vézelay*. His house has now become a gallery of 20th century art. His friend and frequent guest was the writer *Paul Claudel. Maurice Clavel* (1920-1979) dramatist, novelist and philosopher who created the newspaper **Liberation** with *Sartre,* lived first in *Vézelay* and then in *Asquins*. He is buried in the cemetery at *Vézelay. Le Corbusier* (1887-1965) and *Jean Badovici* (1893-1957) passed through and left their mark on the town's buildings. Over a period of 20 years *Violet-Le-Duc* (1814-1879) restored the basilica. *Adolphe Guillon* (1829-1896) painted and sketched sites and characters of *Vézelay. Serge Gainsbourg* chose to spend his final year in *St Père-sous-Vézelay* soaking up the atmosphere – composing and singing in the bar of *Mark Meneau's* famous *L'Espérance*. But it is alleged that he refused to enter the basilica at *Vézelay*, considering himself to be 'unworthy'.

Many living writers and artists have established themselves in the area. What is it that speaks to them all? Like Glastonbury, the *Avallonnais* region attracts men and women of vision – Christian and otherwise. Working back through the layers – long before the eminent residents, the refurbishments, the great Tympanum in the basilica, long before the Crusades, before the pilgrimages, before the arrival of the bones and hair of Mary Magdalene, when "*la colline éternelle*" [the eternal hill] was only grazing ground for sheep, the temple at *Les Fontaines Salées* was drawing the crowds. The members of those crowds no doubt had many differing viewpoints, but their responses to their surroundings – perceived and imagined – were the same. Since Neolithic times the *Avallonnais* area has been identified as a 'portal' to another existence. Together with Glastonbury it shares the reputation of being a place where the veil is thin, dividing the material from the spiritual, the breath of the gods from the cosmic air.

Today, modern pilgrims arrive in coach-loads from all parts of Europe. They wear colourful uniforms and badges. Perhaps they always did. They come to Vézelay, obviously. But they also come to the River *Cure*, stand by the bridge in *Sermizelles* and have outdoor services which involve the use of river water. The river has a reputation for healing properties which extends to the period before Christianity.

Coach-loads of pilgrims also leave *Vézelay* on their way to Compostella. They follow the Cocquilles St. Jacques brass shells embedded in the road, down the hill from the basilica, then they depart. Sometimes they walk or cycle.

It is difficult to know whether the Scorpion Hill had any function during the time of Riothamus. It's possible to see the hill from a long way off. At the very least, therefore, perhaps it had a beacon. But there is no hard evidence to suggest that it was home to anything more than sheep and vines.

There are some other strong similarities between *Avallonnais* and Glastonbury which are worth exploring, but perhaps the most striking is the one which people find most difficult to articulate. They talk about an arcane connection between spirit and element. For those who see it, and feel it, they say that there is a deep mysticism in the landscape itself. There are harmonies and vibrations – a richness of colour and light. Legend isn't only in the wind – it's in the stones, the earth, the water and the fires that herald the spring …

"It flies in the slipstream of the sudden dash of a deer through the fields."

Quite simply, the place was made for Arthur and Arthurian romance. Dion Fortune (1891-1946) would have been completely at home:

> "All about us it [the past] stirs and breathes, quiet but living and watching. We can hear its heart beat if we lay our ear to the earth."[66]

Her spiritual passion was, of course, Glastonbury, but she could just as easily have been talking about *Avallonnais*.

So, *Avallonnais* has the spiritual credentials, but how far does the landscape match the very first quasi-literary description that we have?

Geoffrey of Monmouth's description of a self-sufficient, mystical landscape may be simply classical allusion – his nod to a bucolic idyll. It may also be his foray into an imagined, mythical landscape. But it may not be. Nothing mentioned in his description is beyond the bounds of rationality. In his

Avalon there are no ploughs and no cultivation. The apple trees are thriving in well-trimmed orchards and the vines weigh heavy with fruit, and with no one to tend it all. There is abundant fertility. (For full account see pages 21-22)

Even as the name 'Avalon' could have come originally from an early remembrance of *Avallon,* the actual place where Arthur Riothamus may have ended his fighting career; this description of the area may be an echo of what Arthur Riothamus' soldiers found when they got there. It may well have seemed to them a kind of paradise after the ravages of war. Some of his soldiers may have recovered from their wounds before returning to Britain. There they would have told stories about what they had found in Gaul – descriptions that would be more or less accurate. This then passed into folklore – into the oral tradition from which Geoffrey and others garnered their material.

It is very possible to create a rationale for Geoffrey's deserted Avalon, and apply it to *Avallon*, Burgundy. For example, Arthur's soldiers may well have discovered agricultural land that had been left untended. The fruit (apples and cherries) and vines which typify Burgundy are to be found growing wild throughout the area. They are also cultivated in the lush and fertile land. Without the pesticides and fertilizers, and other modern-day viticultural 'advances' which require activity, there really is no need to do anything much to vines. They require no water, and without present government quotas, would not have needed any pruning. And in any case, in the height of summer, which this obviously was, people never work in the fields by day because it is too hot.

Avallon could have been 'abandoned' because of the arrival of Arthur's bedraggled and bloody troop of vanquished soldiers. They would have been spotted from miles away, and identified as yet another set of 'barbarians'. The only inhabitants left may well have been very elderly. The region still has a name for longevity as a visit to a village cemetery will confirm. The young men could have been conscripted to join what was left of the Roman legion at *Camp Cora,* to protect the Via Agrippa. The women and children could have retreated deep into the impenetrable *Morvan*, whose dark forests would have defeated even the most persistent Hun, as they defeated Hitler.

None of this conjecture proves anything, of course. But it does present the thesis that the *Avallonnais* area of Burgundy has both the mystical and poetic credentials to at least mount a lively challenge to the accepted narrative.

THE RELIGIOUS LANDSCAPE

Celtic religion resonates on every level with the spirit of Arthurian literature. The Celts were connected to their surroundings. Theirs was a religion of sensation and presence – of touch, taste and feel, sound and light. They found and celebrated their gods within nature and natural phenomena. They made music and sang their poetry. They re-created their images in art and sculpture. When they were working and when they travelled, their gods went with them. Before the Four Elements were codified in medieval times, the Celts recognized the mystery of fire in their forges and kilns, in their purifying bonfires and cremations. They visualized the moving air using imagery of birds and flying creatures. They mined the earth, grew their crops and celebrated the harvest and fertility. And above all, they understood the power of water – to cleanse, nourish and to heal. Wells, springs and rivers were sacred places where offerings were made, and miracles wrought. Their many gods and goddesses were elementally charged and worshipped in natural settings.

After the invasion, the Romans adopted sacred Celtic sites as their own and gradually the pantheon of Roman gods and goddesses replaced those of the Celts. There was tolerance towards the religion, although the powerful Druid class was outlawed.

The essence of Celtic religion permeates Arthur's stories. A story can be Celtic without being Arthurian – but not vice versa. A story can even be 'Arthurian' without being about Arthur (*Star Wars, Indiana Jones, Lord of the Rings, Harry Potter*). But in order to have that Arthurian feel – whether spoof 21st century – or never-written-down-fifth century, the story will be unmistakeably Celtic.

We recognise that Arthurian stories have special, identifiable features. They happen in fantastical places deeply connected to natural phenomena and locations which exude their own magic and animism. We expect heroes and villains to use magic weapons against fabulous beasts and foes. We expect the Otherworld to be ever-present, and to find strong druid-type characters who straddle the worlds and use their super-natural arts for good or ill. We know that there will be omens and auguries, and at times a sense of the darkest evil.

We expect questions and conundrums to confound and make mischief with human destiny. There will be strong women, often of fairy origin, and strange parentage, and births and deaths that are unusual, or magical. There will be epic battles that are won through supernatural intervention. We expect our heroes to be bold, valiant and honourable – but above all we expect them to fight and ultimately, to win.

Now most of that has nothing whatsoever to do with Christianity. In fact, the magical and supernatural aspects of Arthurian stories could be deemed heresy from the time of Geoffrey of Monmouth up to the present day. The Christian religion is still decidedly jumpy about 'magic' even after two thousand years. In Geoffrey's time it was nothing less than life-threatening to go 'off-message'. So Geoffrey overcompensates. His Arthur is a Christian Knight – charging around the battlefield with a shield on which there is an image of the Virgin Mary so that he can be constantly reminded of Christianity. He kills in the name of the 'Blessed Virgin'. In Geoffrey's tale and in the stories later to come involving holy quests and grails, Arthur's battles are explained as Christian religious wars. He is a Crusader fighting the Infidel. The story of Arthur 'goes medieval' as soon as religion enters into it – because that was the preoccupation at the time of writing.

The real religious story is very different. By the fifth Century AD the whole of western civilisation was in a state of transition. The authority of the Romans, who had had a profound influence on all aspects of life, was crumbling. The establishment of Christianity was to become one of their most important and abiding legacies. But it didn't happen overnight. In reality, how established had it become by Arthur's time? In other words, how Christian was Arthur? How Celtic? How Roman?

Amongst indigenous tribes fifth century Gaul was probably fundamentally still Celtic/Roman. In Britain the same was probably true. By then, the Romans had contributed their famous pantheon of gods and goddesses, followed by Christianity which was beginning to take hold. Numerous saints – all with their own stories and particular miraculous powers – were edging out the familiar deities without too much intellectual upheaval. Other religions arrived through foreign legionaries and invading 'barbarians', which also had their converts. In all likelihood there were religious 'cells' around Gaul – some centred on small Christian communities; some on local Celtic places and gods of function; some on agricultural seasons or practices; some on war; some on Roman deities. The ancient religious landscape in Burgundy reflects them all.

The old Celtic gods and goddesses – and there were a great many of them, over 400 have been counted – had been adopted and re-named by the Romans, to correspond to their Roman god equivalents. According to Julius Caesar there was an 'elite' set of gods responsible for the main tenets of the Celtic religion. He refers to them by their imposed Roman names:

> *"They worship chiefly the god Mercury; of him there are many symbols, and they regard him as the inventor of all the arts, as the guide of travellers, and as possessing great influence over bargains and*

commerce. After him they worship Apollo and Mars, Jupiter and Minerva. About these they hold much the same beliefs as other nations. Apollo heals diseases, Minerva teaches the elements of industry and the arts, Jupiter rules over the heavens, Mars directs war. All the Gauls assert they are descended from Dispater, their progenitor."

This gives us an idea of the four main preoccupations of the Celts which were:

> The Arts, Travel, Trade and Commerce (Mercury and Minerva)
>
> Health, Healing and Procreation (Apollo)
>
> War and Battle Success (Mars)
>
> The Cult of the Ancestor and the Otherworld (Dispater)

But many Celtic gods and goddesses were considerably less 'grand' than these super-gods. They often had personal, localised names, and had a specific significance and function within both remit and geographical area.

The great influence that the Celts were to exert came through trade and gradual assimilation. Celtic merchants travelled widely taking with them not only their wares, but also their skills, beliefs, knowledge, customs and fashions. These were adopted and absorbed by other indigenous populations because they were seen to be superior to their own, and represented cultural advance. Their Mercury and Minerva-type deities were profoundly important to them as part of a group of special gods for all aspects of art, industry, trade and travel. In Burgundy there are numerous temples to Mercury (to say nothing of the famous Burgundy wine named after him). The temple to Mercury at *Fontenay-près-Vézelay* as previously mentioned, was linked to the production of iron. Other shrines and statues to Mercury in the *Avallonnais* have been found in *Magny, Quarré-les-Tombes, Voutenay-sur-Cure* and *Island* (see Chapter 7), whilst Minerva had a shrine at *St. Moré*.[67]

Of all the gods in the 'Apollo' category of Health, Healing and Procreation, in addition to Taranis, Diana and Venus who were worshipped at *Les Fontaines Salées*, two other important Celtic deities have left their mark on Burgundy: *Borvo* and *Sequana*.

In Gaul there are many wells or springs dedicated to *Borvo*. His name is contained within place names such as *Bourbonne-les-Bains* and *Bourbon-Lancy*. He is known throughout Gaul as a healing god of bubbling water, and is often depicted as a jolly, rotund little man wearing nothing much but a purse and holding an overflowing cup of liquid in one hand, and a bowl of fruit in the other, denoting health and prosperity. There is a mysterious well and cavern dedicated to him, disappearing into the side of the escarpment at *St. Moré* – above the *Grottes d'Arcy*. It is also a site of natural interest as the spring breeding ground of the striking gold and black salamander. It's a bit of a climb. Until the beginning of the last century it was the site of an annual pilgrimage from *Girolles, Sermizelles* and *Givry*.

Another major Celtic healing and fertility cult was discovered in Burgundy at the source of the *Seine* to the north west of *Dijon*. This was dedicated to the goddess Sequana.

Sequana was deemed to be so important that the Romans established the *Fontes Sequanae* and built their temples, shrines and bath houses around the spring and pool, and opened what must have been one of the first spa resorts in Gaul. As a goddess she was ultimately much more 'refined' than Borvo. She is depicted as a high-born woman in a duck-shaped boat – her healing arms stretched out in welcome. She is specifically connected to both healing and fertility as well as the source of the *River Seine*, and only named in relation to that location. She gave her name to the Celtic tribe of the area, the *Sequanae*.

From the many beautifully-carved offerings found at the shrine of *Sequana* it would seem that fertility, family, couples, babies, horses and pets were of central influence and importance to the Celts. And from the thousands of ex votos found there, it would be easy to conclude that the Celts were all obsessed with their health and physical well-being. Their need to procreate successfully and abundantly is also central to Arthur's story.[68]

Warfare was never far from the Celtic heart. Temples and statues to the Roman god Mars were found in *Avallon, Châtel Gérard, Quarré-les-Tombes*, and most importantly on top of *Montmarte*[69] – the great hill overlooking *Avallon* and the valleys of the rivers *Cure* and *Cousin*. Here there were no fewer than four marble statues of Mars discovered, as well as unidentified masculine heads and a full limestone statue of what is described as a *Prêtre* or *Genius* – a high priest. There were the remains of scabbards and swords, and part of an inscription to the god Mars. The foundations and finely painted tile fragments found on top of the hill are consistent with those of a villa as well as a large temple.

Montmarte has a strange atmosphere. I have never been up there alone. It's the only place where I've always taken someone with me. I don't know what I expected to find. I knew that all the statues and the mosaic floors had long been removed. But there are plenty of stones and the remnants of walls to be seen. It's densely wooded apart from the summit which opens out into a grassy area. It's a bit of a climb to get right to the top. The view is only partial because of the trees.

Someone has built an altar up there. Roughly, out of dry stone. There's a wooden cross and collections of dried twigs. It's the kind of wayside shrine that you feel you can contribute to. I found a piece of white marble to add to it. But I'm not sure what it's for – or what it's saying. Is it staking a claim for Christianity on what was once an important pagan site? Is it warding off something evil? There are local legends about people going mad if they spend the night up there …There are the remains of several charcoally fires, so someone braves it.

In the valley of the *Cousin* more than 100 Merovingian *sépultures* were found containing bodies orientated north-south with iron swords and grave goods, all of which add up to this being a most important shrine to the god of war – and incidentally – may give credence to *Montmarte's* candidacy as *Vercingetorix's* last stand against the Romans. Could this have been a lasting memorial to Caesar's victory? Could *Montmarte* be *Alésia?* On his website, *Alésia et Dependances (www.alesia-et-dependances.fr)* Yves de Bermond has some very interesting theories about *Montmarte, Sermizelles* and their topographical features.

The Celts were deeply superstitious. Each stage of their lives was surrounded by the supernatural. The souls of ancestors were ever-present. Malignancy and the power of enemy magic were tangible. The Otherworld was a golden place of rest and material beauty, which was an inspiration and an ultimate destination. It could also break through into the material world and appear in many guises to affect life and the living. Their major festivals followed farming and crop cycles and the changing astronomical seasons. Much later Christianity adopted them as its own. Dispater was the Roman god of the dead – acknowledged as being the Celtic equivalent of the thunder-god, Taranis, as worshipped at *les Fontaines Salées*. The Celts apparently counted time by nights rather than days and believed that they were descended from the god himself. Sometimes he is represented carrying a scroll thought to be the 'Book of Life' symbolising the passage from youth to old age followed by death. He is often accompanied by a three-headed dog[70]. In *Avallonnais* in *Thory,* a statue of Jupiter was found close to the church together with a stone with an inscription to *Diis Pater*.[71] The wheel or book of life represented by Dispater embodied the Celtic belief in reincarnation.

In *Avallon* itself, as previously mentioned, there was said to be a school of Druids:

> *".... des vestiges de constructions gauloises ont fait supposer qu'il avait existé à Aballo un collège de Druides, et que ce collège aurait été l'origine des écoles qui, sous les Romains et encore longtemps après, ont eu une si grande renommée."*[72]

[Translation: ... remains of Gallic buildings led to the supposition that there had been a Druidic school in *Avallon* and that this school may have been the origin of schools which, under the Romans and for long afterwards, had such a great reputation ...]

Caesar has this to say about the Druids' schools:

> "Report says that in the schools of the Druids they learn by heart a great number of verses, and therefore some persons remain twenty years under training........ The cardinal doctrine which they seek to teach is that souls do not die, but after death pass from one to another; and this belief, as the fear of death is thereby cast aside, they hold to be the greatest incentive to valour. Besides this, they have many discussions as touching the stars and their movement, the size of the universe and the earth, the order of nature, the strength and the powers of the immortal gods ..."[73]

The idea of reincarnation is emphasised by Lucan in his *Pharsalia*. He is addressing the Druids:

> "It is you who say that the shades of the dead seek not the silent land of Erebus and the pale halls

of Pluto; rather, you tell us that the same spirit has a body again, elsewhere, and that death, if what you sing is true, is but the mid-point of long life." [74]

Local historians think that the Druids' school in *Avallon* had become a Christian school by the end of the fifth century, and that the church of *Saint-Martin* in *Avallon* was built on the foundations of a temple to Apollo, which *Saint Martin* himself had torn down when he visited the town in 376 AD. However we don't know how far the transition to Christianity progressed when Arthur Riothamus might have visited the region.[75] Neither shall we ever know exactly how much of Gaul had been converted to Christianity by then. However, we know that Celtic/pagan practices were still being continued in the area until the end of the sixth Century because of this edict issued by the diocese of *St. Germain* in *Auxerre*:

> *"il n'est pas permis de célébrer dans les maisons particulières des offrandes privées, ni des veillées pour les fêtes des saints, ni de s'acquitter de voeux parmi les fourrés, ni au pied des arbres sacrés, ni près des sources; [....Et que personne] ne peut se permette aucunement de fabriquer des objets sculptés: soit un pied, soit un bonhomme de bois"* [76]
>
> [Translation: It is not permitted to celebrate offertory services in private houses, nor to hold vigils for Saints' days, nor to take vows either in woods (fourré literally means a thicket), or under sacred trees or near springs; (nor may anyone be permitted in any way to fashion items of sculpture whether this be a foot or a small human wooden effigy.]

Many pagan beliefs existed alongside Christianity. The 'barbarians' brought their own northern Gods. Many of the soldiers in the legions had come from distant parts of the Empire, where the old religions still flourished. The cult of Mithras, for example, was adopted by soldiers who had either come from, or seen service in, the East. There are many similarities between Mithraism and Christianity. It was certainly a forerunner of Christianity and was not discouraged by the Romans.

There are hardly any Christian archaeological finds dating from these times, and none from the *Avallonnais* region. The nearest were in *Auxerre* and *Sens*. But there were three significant Christian monks/saints with strong associations with Burgundy and *Avallon,* who should not go unmentioned when mapping the emergence of Christianity and its connection with Arthur in Gaul.

The first was *St Martin de Tours* who came to the town in 376 to destroy a temple to Apollo then re-consecrate the ground as a Christian site, as previously mentioned. Although almost a century before Arthur Riothamus, *Martin* is a key figure in that he was said to be closely allied with Emperor Maximus. In Geoffrey's **History**, Maximus, who married a British wife, is virtually responsible for the establishment of Brittany after he'd conquered Gaul with his largely British army. According to Geoffrey, Uther Pendragon, Arthur's father and descendant of Maximus, was brought up in Brittany. *St. Martin de Tours'* mission was to convert the pagan tribes of Gaul. In particular he was concerned with the Celtic *Aeduans* who inhabited a large part of what is now northern and central Burgundy, where *Avallon* was a key town. One of the local legends concerning *Martin* is that he discovered and dedicated a fountain in *Asquins* when he paused there with his donkey. Given the involvement between Saint Martin and the Breton royal line, and his sustained connection with *Avallon*, it is conceivable that *Avallon* was well-known to Uther's ancestors and therefore to both Uther and Arthur. Why does Arthur return again and again to Burgundy in Geoffrey's account? The ancient connection between Emperor Maximus and St. Martin may have been the reason.

As a postscript to *St. Martin's* story, some centuries later his body was removed from *Tours* in response to aggressive Viking invasions, and for safety was taken east and ended up in Burgundy in a small village now called *Chablis*. The monks who carried his uncorrupted body around Gaul in a special painted wooden trunk, had thoughtfully brought with them some vine stock from the Loire valley. This stock was the basis for the production of the famous white Burgundy wine.

The second saint is *St. Germanus* – or *St. Germain* – of *Auxerre,* 378? – 448. *Germanus* is very important. He is mentioned extensively in Geoffrey's **History**, and was also a very real historical figure. His life is recorded by Constantius of Lyon. He is therefore one of the key elements of Geoffrey's account that provides evidence of a date for Arthur.

Germanus was a devout follower of *St. Martin* and was born into a noble family in *Auxerre* – under fifty miles away from *Avallon,* due north on the Via Agrippa. *Auxerre*

*(*Autessiodurum) had been founded by the Romans in the first century and was an important walled city used as a stronghold against the barbarian invasions. Following his schooling which is thought to have been in *Avallon, Autun* and *Rome*, Germanus spent some time as a soldier. He became Bishop of *Auxerre* in 418. He was a hands-on defender of religion and actively joined in battles and peace negotiations. He is mentioned with the Bishop of *Troyes*, in Geoffrey's **History** as part of his account of Vortigern's "Halleluja" victory over the Saxons at St Albans in England. *Germanus* went there in 430, and again in 447, to fight the 'hideous dragon of Pelagianism' – a heresy which had its roots in England and travelled as far as the Holy Land, which questioned the authority of priests and the Pope.

In Gaul he is famously remembered for his part in subduing the warlike inclinations of King *Goar* who was sent to quash the rebellion in Brittany against Aëtius. *Germanus* fearlessly held on to the bridle of *Goar's* horse until *Goar* recognised the error of his barbaric ways and negotiated a peaceful settlement of the dispute.

Germanus is not associated with any particular saintly specialisation, but is often linked with other saints such as *Lupus* of *Troyes, Aignan* of *Orleans* and *Geneviève* of *Paris*. He was known for his good sense, valour and for bringing people together. There are 60 or more parishes of *Saint Germain* in *Haut* and *Bas Normandie* – probably named after him when he stopped on his journeys to England.

When he retired he built a monastery on the *'rive droite'* of the River *Yonne*, at *Auxerre* – the first monastery of the

Auxerre diocese – where he founded an evangelistic order. When he died in *Ravennes* his corpse was transported back to *Auxerre*, coming through *Avallon,* accompanied by five *'pieuses femmes'* (pious women) – three of whom died on the Via Agrippa, were made saints and gave their names to the villages close by: *Ste. Magnance, Sainte-Pallaye,* and *Escollives-Sainte-Camille.*

The third saint is Saint Patrick, who entered holy orders at the monastery in *Auxerre.* He was made a bishop by *Germanus.* Patrick was born in Scotland, captured by pirates and taken to Ireland from where he eventually escaped to Gaul. It was *Germanus* who sent him back to Ireland in 432 on his evangelical mission. Many Irish monks came to *Auxerre* in particular as a result. The famous 'peregrinations' of the Irish walkabout monks brought them to Burgundy with their own brand of Celtic Christianity – which was eventually suppressed by Rome. Significantly, the bones of St. Patrick were 'discovered' in Glastonbury, at around the same time as King Arthur and Guinevere's remains were also discovered.

These three pioneering monks/saints had great influence over the important kings and military leaders of Britain. What is significant, therefore, are the connections and links forged over a period of some 150 years – the period that corresponds with the rise of Arthur's ancestors, and quite possibly the birth of Arthur himself. All three had knowledge of *Avallon.* *Germanus* in particular had thorough knowledge of Britain, and may well have been alive when Arthur was born. Is it conceivable that Arthur's obsession with Burgundy was fuelled by these long-term, established connections with his ancestors?

THE ESOTERIC LANDSCAPE

Was there an esoteric landscape to *Avallonnais* in the fifth century – some kind of 'special knowledge' focused on the area around *Avallon* that was accessible only to initiates and members of a select group that worshipped or held sectarian beliefs in a higher power? We know about the earlier presence of the Druids and their school, the *Mithraic* influence and the importance of *Les Fontaines Salées*. Were there any other '*cultes*'?

Here we must leap forwards about 400 years. We know that legend has *Girart de Roussillon* sending the *Vézelay* monk *Badilon* to *Aix-en-Provence* in order to 'rescue' the corpse of Mary Magdalene from the invading Saracens, in around 880 AD. And that after many tribulations – including having to stop off at *Nîmes* on the way back to cut her into smaller, more transportable pieces – *Badilon* eventually reached *Vézelay*, and thereafter the Cult of Mary Magdalene grew up with the new abbey at the top of the Scorpion Hill.[77] Historically it is confirmed that relics of Mary Magdalene were brought to *Vézelay*, and that they were verified as such by Pope Léon XI in 1050[78].

There are many legends relating to Mary Magdalene – and her body. At least three other centres in western Europe claimed to have Mary's corpse – or bits of her. In another version, *Badilon* went to Jerusalem to fetch her, and from there brought her back to *Girart* in *Vézelay* together with her sister Martha and her brother Lazarus. In this legend *Girart* also presented Lazarus' corpse to the church in *Avallon*. In

The Bible, Jesus raises Lazarus from the dead. The Bishop of *Autun* was furious about Lazarus, as he thought he had him in his church... But is there an echo of Arthur in the Lazarus story?

Yet another legend suggests that in an attempt to get rid of them all in one fell swoop, a boatload of Christian super-saints was launched from the Holy Land in AD 48 without any oars, containing amongst others, Lazarus, Mary Magdalene, Martha and Joseph of Arimathea. They were left to drift through the Mediterranean and finally ended up in the port of *Marseilles*, from where they travelled north. Mary Magdalene and her siblings stayed in Burgundy, and Joseph of Arimathea famously went on to England ... to Glastonbury.

Some claim that Mary Magdalene's popularity was greater than the Virgin Mary's at one time. Her shrine at *Vézelay* was visited by royalty and wealthy merchants from all over Europe. They left valuable gifts, and legacies of property and land as far away as Italy, and the Abbey became one of the richest in Christendom. The cult of Mary Magdalene, together with her relics, made the town of *Vézelay* famous for more than two hundred years. But that was all much, much later.

What is interesting is the palpable link between Avallon and Glastonbury, via the legends of Mary Magdalene, Lazarus and Joseph of Arimathea.

There are so few sources anywhere that mention King Arthur and Avallon in France together, that I feel almost duty-bound to give even the most far-fetched theory a brief nod of recognition, before moving swiftly on.

Following the runaway success in 2003 of the popular novel, **The Da Vinci Code** by Dan Brown, many writers have exploited the central idea of a Catholic Church conspiracy to cover-up a marriage between Mary Magdalene and Jesus, for their own purposes. At the fanciful end of the fallout from Dan Brown's fiction, it was never going to be long before King Arthur entered the frame. More than one writer has traced Arthur's 'ancestry' back through to the Merovingians, via the "Fisher Kings" to Mary Magdalene. And in one case the link arrives swiftly in Burgundy, back to the female members of a "House del Acqs" and in particular to King Arthur's mother "Ygerna del Acqs, daughter of Queen Viviane of Avallon in Burgundy".[79]

There has never been a "House del Acqs" in Avallon. There has never been a king or queen of Avallon, so far as anyone knows. In Arthur Riothamus' times there were only those kings of Burgundy with names mostly beginning with 'G', and none of those was married to a "Viviane of Avallon".

What is interesting, though, is that once again within these legends and fantasies there are resonances with place, linking Avallon in Burgundy with Arthur and his parentage.

And what seems most significant in the whole of this section are the similar expressions of esoteric ideas – and even the fact that they have arisen at all – between Avallon/Vézelay and Glastonbury.

The esoteric signs and symbols of alchemy, and the mathematics of master builders and masons in the area, came into their own much later, when the basilica at *Vézelay* was being built from 1100s onwards. Around *Avallon* there are other notable examples such as the *Château de Chastenay* – formerly the *Château du Lys* – at *Arcy-sur-Cure* which is claimed by *Monsieur le comte de LA VARENDE* to have been in his family, providing shelter for the passing *Compostella* pilgrims, since 1086.[80]

The ancient Celtic cult of the apple is worth exploring because of its association with the name *Avallon* and, according to *Jacques BONNET* in his article, *"Le Site Sacré de Vézelay",* because the symbol of goddess *Rigani* (*La Morrigan* – 'Morgen' see page 68) was three apples in a triangle.

The Crypt of the Archaeological Museum in *Dijon* has been given over to the Roman finds from the city and surrounding area, and most importantly to the finds from the discovery of the *Fontes Sequanae* site at the source of the *Seine*. The collection of *ex voto* in stone, wood and bronze is vast and comprehensive. It is possible to tell, for example, the commonest ailments and diseases of the pilgrims who came to the shrine, which makes a fascinating study in its own right.

However, amongst all the body parts there are iconic sculptures depicting two arms raised high with hands holding together *'un fruit rond'*. There are several versions of this symbolic pose. There are also numerous other representations of hands and figures holding the round fruits, which closely resemble apples. Some of the exhibits are catalogued not as fruits, but as breasts, even though some exhibits just show a single spherical shape, or three or five 'breasts' in a row. These could all be representations of apples. The compiler admits to being uncertain of these interpretations.[81]

M. Bonnet goes further with his point about the triangle of apples. Using the life of *Girart de Roussillon* (the historical one), he compares the three apples with the sites of the three Abbeys founded by *Girart* and his wife, *Berthe*: *Vézelay*, *Pothières* and *Flavigny*. He maintains that the third of these sites, *Flavigny*, although not mentioned in the **Chanson de Geste**, was lost by *Girart* in battle with *Charles le Chauve* [Charles the bald]. He presents a diagram showing that *Pothières* and *Flavigny* are on the same line of longitude (4' 33) – or near as damn it. And that *Avallon/Vézelay* and *Flavigny* are on the same line of latitude (47'30), thus creating a right-angled triangle between the three abbeys. The *Fontes Sequanae* are also on this latitude. These three sites are, of course, ancient Celtic sites adopted first by the Romans, then by Christians.

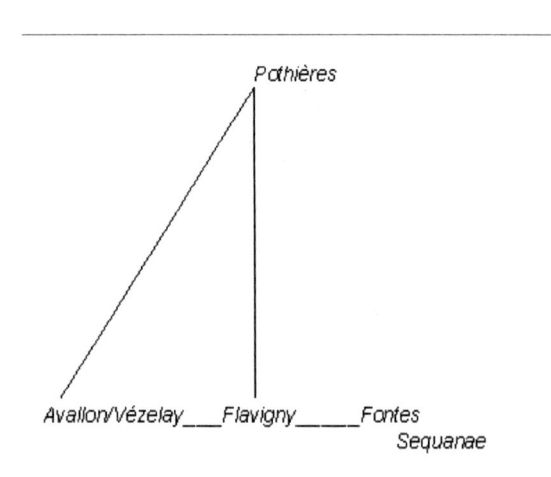

```
                    Pothières
                    /|
                   / |
                  /  |
                 /   |
                /    |
               /     |
              /      |
             /       |
            /        |
           /         |
          /          |
Avallon/Vézelay___Flavigny_____Fontes
                               Sequanae
```

But then he draws the comparison with Glastonbury and Stonehenge in England, which rather strangely, also share the same latitude as each other. It remains a mystery as to how these sites related to each other with such precision mathematically, and what that signified. Would Arthur have been aware of these esoteric rules – and would he have known about their existence and application in Gaul? Would he have made a point of visiting these sites in Burgundy? And what was the cult of the apple anyway? Why were apples so special to the Celts/Romans? As opposed to say, grapes or cherries? Why were there so many stone carvings showing apples held aloft in celebration, as if being offered to the sun? Would Arthur have known the answer to that? And would he therefore have viewed Avallon as a deeply significant place in its own right because of its name?

There is perhaps one more strange coincidence concerning place names that is worth exploring. Driving back to *Avallon* from the TGV railway station at *Montbard* there is a moment when you come over the brow of a hill and look down across a view in which several rounded and distinctive hills feature in an otherwise flat plain. It has always struck me how very similar this landscape is to the view of the hills in Somerset, England, around Glastonbury, which you can see when you come down from the Mendip hills. Even the colours and the light and the patchwork patterns of the fields are similar.

This is not particularly extraordinary in itself. However, I was invited to explore what is thought to be a fortified Neolithic site near the little medieval walled town of *Montréal*. My guides were John Goodall and Cynthia Gayneau who have made an amateur study of Roman and pre-Roman sites in Burgundy. I was not sure where we were going except up one of those rounded hills called *Montagne de Montfault*. They presented me with a copy of a booklet written mostly by *Bernard Fèvre* for *Association Alexandre Parat*. The booklet and the thesis it contained concern yet another alternative proposal for the site of *Alésia* – where

Caesar laid siege to *Vercingetorix*. But, the *Montagne de Montfault* I discovered, is one of two hills – the other hill is known as the *Montagne de Verre* – **the Glass Mountain.** At its summit there are indeed what look like the foundations of a very sizeable ancient settlement, including massively thick walls running around the hill in a circle providing what must have been an almost impenetrable defence barrier. *Bernard Fèvre* spent his lifetime trying to get the authorities to take his thesis seriously. Official archaeological sources state cautiously that the ancient origin of the foundations is 'not proven'.[82] But for my purpose, the discovery of a 'Glass Mountain' in the *Avallonnais* area was rather extraordinary. Later on studying the map, I also discovered that the Glass Mountain is on the same line of latitude as the officially accepted site of *Alésia* to the east, at *Alise-Sainte-Reine*, **and** as another alternative site to the west at *Montmarte/Sermizelles*.

If the French *Avallon* originally provided the name Avalon in Arthurian literature, could the French 'Glass Mountain' have originally been connected with 'Glastonbury'?

Astrologically speaking there are two interesting points about the *Avallonnais* – both of them revealed by the rise of *Vézelay* and the widespread takeover of Christianity.

The hill on which *Vézelay* was founded has been called *Le Mont Scorpion,* certainly since the Vikings were said to have reached the area. In the fifth century it must be remembered that the hill was simply grazing lands with vines on the south-eastern slopes. There is no reliable scientific or archaeological evidence to suggest that there was any building or land-working of any religious significance up that hill until about 1100. Everything that was sacred from Neolithic times, through the Celts, Romans and early Christian eras, developed around *les Fontaines Salées* – some three kilometres from the hill, down in the valley of the *River Cure* and some distance from what is now *St. Père*.[83]

The reason why the hill is called *Le Mont Scorpion* has attracted much interest amongst those of an esoteric persuasion. On a superficial level, its unusual elongated topography suggests the shape of a scorpion. There are many vantage points in the surrounding undulating countryside that offer the chance to witness this. As far as I can ascertain there are no theories or theses to suggest that there is a full-blown 'Avallon Zodiac' as was developed around Glastonbury back in the 1960s, for example. But the characteristics of the sign of the Scorpion have certainly been applied to *Vézelay* with its 'passionate' and violent history of conflict between the Abbey, the Counts of *Nevers*, and the town burgesses. This struggle for power between the Bishops, Abbots and Lords of the Manor is another common theme between Glastonbury and Wells in Somerset.

Both Glastonbury Tor and *Le Mont Scorpion* have been the subject of maps and charts showing the paths of 'cosmic energy' and 'currents' of various phenomena. Oddly though, the representation of the Scorpion in the Zodiac as depicted on the famous tympanum in the narthex of the basilica is not the familiar image of the arachnid at all. The sign of Scorpio is depicted as an eight-legged camel – the first six legs being scaly – with the head of a goat or dog.

What is fascinating, however, is that just as John Mitchell in his book *"New Light on the Ancient Mystery of Glastonbury"* explores the notion of the Plough (Big Dipper) constellation and the "seven island stars of Arthur the Great Bear" in the landscape around Glastonbury, a similar thesis has arisen around significant and ancient sites in Burgundy, including *Vézelay/Les Fontaines Salées.*

Allegedly, the druids re-created the constellations in the landscape by founding their most sacred land sites based on the patterns in the stars. There is a Normandy 'Plough' and also one in the *Auvergne*. The Burgundy Plough is now based on Christian sites which were, before that era, sites of ancient druidical worship. [84]

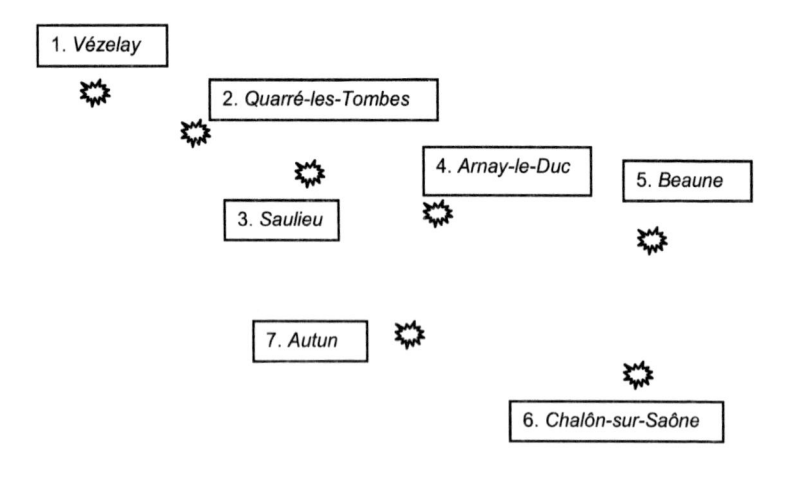

1. Vézelay
2. Quarré-les-Tombes
3. Saulieu
4. Arnay-le-Duc
5. Beaune
7. Autun
6. Chalôn-sur-Saône

1. *Vézelay/Les Fontaines Salées* – The basilica/the mineral springs near *St. Père*

2. *Quarré-les-Tombes* – The Church of St. George famous for the large number of Merovingian sarcophaguses discovered on or nearby the church, and a few kilometres from the dolmen at the *Abbey Pierre-qui-Vire* and the site of the battle locally known as 'Champculan'.

3. *Saulieu* – The church of *Saint Andoche* on the site of an ancient Sun Temple and thought to be a seat of druidic learning

4. *Arnay-le-Duc* – The church of *Saint Laurent* a dependency of the *Abbey of Saint Benigne of Dijon*

5. *Beaune* – The basilica of *Notre Dame de Beaune* on the site of a Temple to Belenus – Celtic equivalent of Apollo – later famed for the 'black madonna' and Knights Templar connections

6. *Châlon-sur-Saône* – The Cathedral of *Saint Vincent* of *Châlon* known as '*Cabillonum*' at the time of the *Aeduan* tribe who used the town as a commercial centre

7. *Autun* – The Cathedral of *Saint Lazare* (the rival to *Avallon* as guardian of Lazurus' corpse). Autun is famous as the new city built by the Romans for the *Aeduan* tribe to replace their oppidum on *Mount Beuvray*, their capital *Bibracte*. *Autun* was built to rival Rome in its splendour. It is also the site of Arthur's final battle in Gaul, according to Geoffrey of Monmouth.

Traditionally 'Arcturus', the star representing King Arthur – the Bear himself – is a bright star, found by extending the 'handle' of the plough in the alignment of the first two stars.

When we do the same with the Burgundy Plough – and extend the line through *Quarré-les-Tombes* to *Vézelay* and onward, the 'Arcturus' star is located ... at *Chartres*.

In the fifth century *Chartres* Cathedral was not, of course, built. But the place remains one of the most esoteric and mystical sites in Christendom.

7
AVALLON – THE FINAL RESTING PLACE

"The grave of Arthur is nowhere beheld, whence ancient
songs fable that he is still to come."
William of Malmesbury

AUTUN AND THE BATTLE OF SAUSSY
THE FINAL CONFLICT IN GAUL

According to Geoffrey of Monmouth in his **History,** King Arthur fought a decisive battle against the Romans, outside the city of *Autun* in 'a valley called *Saussy.*'[85] This was his final conflict in Gaul. But Geoffrey's account is patently not describing Arthur Riothamus' final conflict at *Bourges* against the Visigoths. Therefore, this is a major dissimilarity between fact and fiction which deserves to be looked at.

The city of *Autun* is in the heart of present-day Burgundy, about 80 kilometres due south-east from *Avallon* on the Via Agrippa. Geoffrey's choice of *Autun* is a feasible location for a battle in the fifth century involving Romans. *Autun* was purpose-built by them and completed in the second century, and proved so irresistible to the *Aeduan* tribe, that they left their 'oppidum' at *Bibracte*, and moved there – lock, stock and barrel. It was a vast, fabulous city by all accounts, and had a college, a theatre, monumental gates and a temple to Janus. You can still see the grandeur of the Roman buildings – the remains of the temple, and the great amphitheatre which is still used for pageants in the summer tourist season. It is a great pity though, that a football pitch has been constructed almost inside the amphitheatre, and that the city ring road scarcely gives it breathing space.

What is not easy to comprehend, is where Geoffrey found his information about *Autun,* and about the other towns and cities in Burgundy, and their geographical relationship to each other. Arthur Riothamus would have known *Autun* by repute as the greatest city in the region, as 'the sister and rival of Rome'. In a world where there were no maps, only stars as navigational aids, the number of 'marching days' the only distance guide, and the number of 'passing nights' as the only measure of time, it's astonishing that warring armies ever managed to locate each other at all.

We can't perceive the world as Geoffrey did when he wrote his **History.** All the shapes that are so familiar to us now – the British Isles – Europe – the Holy Land – Italy – Greece and the Mediterranean Sea – forming a major part of our perception and sense of orientation – were not embedded in Geoffrey's consciousness in the same way at all. So how did he know about the relationship between, for example, *Langres* and *Autun* and *Paris*? Was it from reading the classics? Or from the tales of merchants, pilgrims, and soldiers returning home from the early Crusades? We have to assume that if he really spoke with authority about these places, then he must have been in possession of an ancient written record – an eyewitness document verifying some associated battle that he could use as a basis for the story of a great Arthurian victory. For Arthur Riothamus, finding the enemy could have been even more difficult, but at least a few Romans were still around to ask.

But Autun is not where the battle took place, according to Geoffrey. It happened in a valley called *Saussy*. Or *Siesia, Assnessia* or *Sessoyne,* depending on which manuscript you read. In his translation of **History**, Lewis Thorpe gives us an extended footnote opting firmly for what has been called "an obscure place thirty-five miles south-west of *Langres* named *Saussy,* on the way to *Autun*".

Anyone who has ever travelled in France will know how big the country is. A large marching army could probably cover a maximum distance of 30 kilometres a day. The reality of the logistics in Geoffrey's story of the battle of *Saussy* (if he meant that *Saussy* and there isn't any other 'Saussy' or any other variant spelling of it anywhere near *Autun*), the campaign strategies, the to-ing and fro-ing to *Paris*, the routes taken and the ground covered, are all suspect.

To begin with, Geoffrey's account tells us that King Arthur and his army were marching from *Barfleur,* in what is now Normandy, to *Autun* where the Romans were expected to be. The problem is that *Autun* is some 655 kilometres from *Barfleur,* and the route between them goes nowhere near where he mentions the ensuing conflict took place. The route does not cross the *River Aube*, or pass through *Langres,* or the obscure little village of *Saussy,* which is off any existing Roman route and in the middle of nowhere. Even if *Saussy* had existed in the fifth century, how on earth would Geoffrey of Monmouth or Arthur have heard about it? And if they had heard about it, how would anybody have found it to fight a battle in?

It was difficult enough finding it in the car, with a large-scale map. It's the kind of place that looks as if it was deserted just before the onset of WW1. There were probably more cows than humans. The commune had, however, put up a useful map indicating country walks in the area.

In reality, anyone marching an army from *Barfleur* to *Autun* would have gone via *Paris* (Lutècia*)* and the Via Agrippa, and it would have taken them, at the very least, three weeks. Arthur would have marched them through *Auxerre* and *Avallon*, and then either continued on the Via Agrippa for the last 80 kilometres from *Avallon*, or else taken the Julian Apostat secondary road across the *Morvan* via *Les Fontaines Salées, St. Germain des Champs* and *Quarré-les-Tombes*.

Geoffrey's account of the Romans' manoeuvres are forgivably eccentric. He explains that Lucius Hiberius (a wholly 'fictitious' Roman 'Procurator') had already reached the *River Aube* – coming out (from where?) to meet Arthur's army with an enormous force eager to engage in battle. The first skirmishes took place and then Lucius marched his army into *Langres*. [Although in one manuscript[86] it is referred to as 'Augustudunum' the Roman name of *Autun* not *Langres*, which would have been known as *'Langones'*.] Arthur then outflanked him – by-passed *Langres* on his left and went south and waited for Lucius in a valley called *Saussy* 'through which Lucius would have to pass'.

Saussy is en route to nowhere. Marching from *Langres* to *Autun* would have taken almost six days, and passing through *Saussy* would have required a considerable detour. Saussy would not have been part of the itinerary. The way he tells it, Geoffrey would have us believe that *Langres, Saussy* and *Autun* were within spitting distance of each other. Taking prisoners back to *Paris* from the battlefield would have been a 20-day round trip. It is astonishing that although the distances are impracticable, Geoffrey did get the general sense of direction right, and the relationship between the three is at least plausible. But the geography can't really be reconciled with the imagination, and the whole *Langres, Saussy* and *Autun* events, together with the battle, seem very improbable.

So I tried to find alternative locations to the one put forward by Lewis Thorpe, closer to *Autun* and on either the Via Agrippa or the secondary Roman road across the Morvan. But there just aren't any. No 'real' battles, no 'real' places that have any resemblance to the name 'Saussy'.

For our purposes, *Autun* and the story of Arthur's final campaign in Gaul is a conundrum. There was, of course, a 'real' battle of *Soissons* which took place in 486 AD between Merovingian King Clovis – the first 'king' of France and sometime ally of Riothamus, and the Romans led by Syagrius, son of Aegidius – also sometime ally of Riothamus. This was the final Roman conflict after which the Frankish kingdom expanded to become much of what is now France. So, the conflict itself could have been significant for Arthur Riothamus – either way. If he had fought on the side of the Franks, then he would be fighting against the Romans – and in particular, against Syagrius, the Roman who had let him down at *Bourges*. Which begins to look a lot more feasible.

Could Arthur Riothamus have taken part in the battle of **Soissons**? Are these the echoes that Geoffrey used to weave his own story around the fictitious 'Lucius Hiberius'? He would have known about three possible 'battles of *Soissons*'

– the one mentioned above, one in 718 AD and yet another in 923 AD. The name of *Soissons* in Gaul would certainly have had resonances for Geoffrey.

If the battle of *Soissons* equates with the battle of *Saussy*, then where did the subsequent battle of 'Camblan' (traditionally located beside the River Camel in Cornwall) take place? Who would Arthur Riothamus have as an enemy the equivalent of Mordred, in Gaul? Does anyone 'real' fit the bill?

In Geoffrey Ashe's[87] account of Arthur Riothamus' retreat from *Bourges* Riothamus has a 'real' enemy. The man who betrayed his position was an imperial prefect in Gaul called Arvandus. And as we know already, the historical **Chronicle of Anjou** refers to Arthur's nephew as 'Morvandus'. Arvandus was impeached by the Senate in Rome because of his treasonous support of the Visigoths and their King Euric, against the Britons, Franks and Burgundians. He sneered at the Emperor, betrayed the position of the British army, and encouraged Euric to 'detach the Burgundians from their Roman alliance and carve up Gaul with them."[88] Arvandus was first sentenced to death, then banished from Rome. Is it possible that he came back to the Morvan to fight one further battle with Riothamus?

If Arthur eventually fell in Burgundy – as a result of a battle – or as a result of injury or old age, then there are plenty of places which might have become his final resting place.

A CHRISTIAN BURIAL?

As you might expect from an area that has been inhabited since antiquity, bodies have been discovered all over Burgundy. But most importantly, amongst them are bodies from the right era, the fifth century AD.

In his book "**The Discovery of King Arthur**" Geoffrey Ashe sums up the possibilities concerning Arthur's final resting place according to literature:

> ".... There are two main notions: one, that he is in Avalon ..... the other, that he lies asleep in a cave."

So, in *Avallon,* where would you bury Arthur, fabulous King of the Britons? That, of course, depends on who buried him and what was their religion – and what was Arthur's.

If Arthur were Christian, then we'd be looking for consecrated ground on the site of a very early Christian church. There is evidence that only one of the churches in Avallon itself is sufficiently ancient. In 1861 a tiny cave or chapel was discovered dug into the rock, underneath the choir of the *Eglise Saint-Lazare* – which was allegedly founded by *Girart de Roussillon* at approximately the same time as *Vézelay*. The entrance to the chapel faced east – high on the ramparts – looking out over the Morvan. Based on the layer principle, this little chapel, forgotten for centuries, might have been the crypt of the first Christian church.[89] Or it might not. It could have contained the original relics of *Saint Lazare* – but no one knows for sure. If Girart never possessed the body of Lazurus in the first place, then whose relics were given to the church in *Avallon* – when the 'real' ones went to *Autun*? Does the story of the man who was brought back to life by Jesus have any resonances that might suggest it was Arthur's body?

The only other reference to a Christian building in the *Avallonnais* is that chapel dedicated to *Jean-Baptiste* – built at *Les Fontaines Salées* during the fifth century. To re-cap for a moment. This most sacred site dating from Neolithic times provides evidence not only of mineral helium springs and the processes used to extract salt through the ages, but it also reveals archaeological evidence of a sequence of religious history: Celtic healing sanctuary; Gallo-Roman Temple; Roman baths; Christian chapel; probable site of ancient monastery for women founded by *Girart de Roussillon*. The particular location of the ruins of the chapel is referred to under the name of, 'sancti Johannes in loco qui Vetus Viceliacus cognominatur' which confirms not only the early Christian connection, but also the name from which *Vézelay* was taken.[90] The area is now referred to as *Corvée Saint Jean* and the foundations are in the middle of a cultivated field just north of *Les Fontaines Salées*.

Logically, there is no reason why this little chapel should have been built at all – given that the 'barbarians' were supposed to be rampaging through Burgundy at this time, destroying everything in their path. *René Louis* who was central to the re-discovery of *Les Fontaines Salées,* was the first to explore the foundations in 1935 and again in 1936. He describes a building 30m X 9m divided into three sections, the whole being surrounded by a wall. He thought that there were two phases of building – one much earlier than the other, because of two different foundation layers. The bottom and therefore the oldest layer is *"remblai"* – a small-grade gravel quarried locally and still used in traditional building in the Morvan today. Above that there is a layer of cinder subsoil. In the subsoil he discovered various ceramic fragments, fibulae, a bronze knife and dated coins giving usage up until the fifth century. He called it a

> *"vaste sanctuaire des deux premiers siècles sur les ruines duquel fut construit peut-être dès le IVe siècle un oratoire dédié à Saint Jean-Baptiste."* [91]
> [Translation: a large sanctuary from the first two centuries on the ruins of which was built, perhaps in the fourth century, an oratory dedicated to John the Baptist]

So why on earth did someone go to the trouble of building this special edifice out of the ruins of an ancient sanctuary in those uncertain times? Aerial photographs of the site taken in 1989 show two routes bordering the building, one of which is a pathway leading to a fording place across the River *Cure,* mentioned in several texts, called *Gué de Saint-Jean*. On the *'rive droite'* of the *Cure* was the secondary Roman road named after Julien l'Apostat, which crossed the *Morvan* via *Saint-Germain-des-Champs, Quarré-les-Tombes,* and eventually led to *Autun*. Given the large number of finds suggesting active usage until the end of the fifth century, together with its close proximity to a river crossing and major route, we may be looking at a pilgrimage site. But whatever the truth of the matter, this site has the credentials to make it a front-runner as King Arthur's purpose-built, final, Christian, resting place.

THE LITTLE FINGER OF GARGANTUA

In the tradition of the Celts, the greatest kings were buried beneath standing stones, as a lasting memorial. In Geoffrey's *History,* both Aurelius Ambrosius and Uther Pendragon were buried beneath Stonehenge.

In *Avallon* there is one hidden standing stone – linked to Merlin and Arthur by the Breton legends of *'Gargantua'*. It is called *'Petit doigt de Gargantua'*, and is not to be found on any tourist maps. I came across it in a reprint of Ernest Petit's 1867, *'Avallon et Avallonnais – Etude Historique'*. He says that it rises to a total height of seven metres and that it holds a prominent position within a natural amphitheatre of rock, close to the bridge over the *River Cousin,* and that it was put there by human hand in an era when such stones were the object of cult worship. I had high hopes. But Ernest was being a little extravagant with the truth, and the search for the actual location of *Gargantua's* digit proved problematic.

On our fifth attempt, with the help of my friend Patrice Deschamps, we finally located a gentleman, who for his own future peace shall remain nameless, who remembered playing around it as a child and indicated that it was somewhere up on the densely wooded cliff behind his house. It was a tough climb. We kept expecting to see the Digit towering over us through the trees. I had visited a magnificent standing stone in Brittany some years before which suddenly loomed up out of the middle of a forest. I was imagining that we'd have a similar experience. Seven metres is very high. In fact, it turned out to be nothing like that. It was not what I would call a real standing stone at all – more like an overgrown triangulation point built on to a rocky outcrop. The total height from the base of the outcrop might be seven metres, but the built Digit – the bit that was 'placed there by human hand' was scarcely more than a metre high. The place was covered in thorny thicket and had absolutely no otherworldly atmosphere. It might have been more mysterious before the municipal camp site was built, nearby. And before the pylons and overhead electricity cables. This was truly an imagination crash.

THE 'ISLAND' OF AVALLON

Believe it or not, there is a village called *Island* right in the middle of the *Avallonnais*. This is surprising on a number of counts. Etymologically speaking, it is a very strange name for a village in France. It has a Germanic root. The most usual name meaning an island would be *Isle* – and there are many *Isles* in Burgundy.

Interestingly enough, the direct route from *Bourges* to *Avallon* passes through Island. From the Loire crossing at *La Charité*, the road leads via *Clamecy*, through what is now *St. Père*, past the *Chapelle du Saulce* (chapel of the willows) and thence through the village of *Island*, before reaching *Avallon*.

In fact, the correct name of the village is *Island-le-Saulçois* – the willow island – and it spreads out over several small hamlets covering a vast watery, wooded area of wells and interconnecting springs, which make it liable to flooding. It is about three miles from *Avallon* and almost exactly midway between *Avallon* and *Les Fontaines Salées*. In the 12th century it was written as *Ielent* which probably sounded close to present day pronunciation.[92] No one really seems to know why the village is called *Island.* Once again though, someone thought 'it was named after that place in England – the Island of Avalon ...' One source suggested that it was named after a Celtic princess called *Iselindis* – but I can find no trace of her. An explanation was offered that local legend refers to her as being connected with, or confused with *Iseult* – and a 'Grail story'... Is this a 'hazy memory' of something?

We know that *Island* is ancient because of the numerous Gallo-Roman finds that have been discovered there: a complete bronze torque, some rings and fibulae, and bracelets. Close to the church the foundations of a large Roman villa were discovered with quantities of ceramic tiles, mosaic tiles, pottery, shards of amphorae, bass-relief figures and coins. There was also a bronze statue of Mercury. A tumulus containing human remains may have been in *Island,* but it could have been in *Pontaubert* or *Vault-de-Lugny* instead. The records are unreliable. There was apparently

> *"un dolmen détruit il y a 25 années."*
> [Translation: a dolmen which was destroyed twenty-five years ago.] This was recorded in an archaeological pamphlet dated 1873.[93]

I wish there were more. *Island* was certainly there at the time of Arthur Riothamus. It was certainly on the main route to *Avallon* from the *Loire* – so he, and what was left of his soldiers, could have passed through it. But whether there is anything much more significant about *Island* – and whether it could be a contender as Arthur's place of burial – is anybody's guess.

The *Chapelle du Saulce* is obviously of interest. Except, that it is of course far too late to have any Arthurian connections in its present form. It was dated as 1209 by the abbot *Baudiau,* and is considered to be one of the finest chapels still standing of the Order of the Knights Templar.

It was built on an earlier site beside a holy well – now dedicated to *Sainte-Anne,* which was in ancient times, a pilgrimage destination. It also seems likely that the site was an important centre before then. There is evidence of an agricultural community there and a vast lake dating from the Middle Ages. This lake was restored in 1830, but sadly there is no evidence of it left.[94] The *Chapelle* is now privately owned, at the end of a private road, and has been completely renovated as a dwelling.

MEROVINGIAN CEMETERIES, SARCOPHAGUSES AND QUARRIES

We can't answer the question of what religion was practised in the mid – late 5th century, with any certainty. Therefore we need to recapitulate what we have learned about the Celts and Romans, with specific reference to how the Merovingians dealt with their dead.

If Arthur and the person or persons who buried him were still of the old, pagan Celtic/Roman religion, then we could be looking for something altogether different. A straightforward burial might not have been the only option. The Celts and Romans cremated their dead and placed their ashes in vases in necropoli. Some Celts buried their dead in shallow graves beside flowing water, so that their bodies would eventually be borne away. They also floated them down sacred rivers in hollowed tree-trunks, or placed them in caves beside fountains, or shrines. Later, they buried bodies in elaborate graves beneath tumuli with grave goods, valuable possessions and necessities for their otherworldly journey. This often included a cart or wagon. Later still, the graves of many affluent citizens were marked by wayside stones, showing the profession of the deceased and with a short inscription. The Romans built fine mausoleums for their celebrated dead.

According to the *Carte Archéologique de la Gaule* for the Department of the *Yonne* there are examples of all of these in and around *Avallon*. The most famous (and fabulous) example of the Celtic 'wagon' burial is the grave of the Lady, or Princess of *Vix*. It contained the Treasure of *Vix* – the glory of which is the massive '*Vix Crater*' – the largest Greek bronze vase surviving today. It could contain 1,100 litres of wine and is 1.64m high. This truly spectacular artefact can be seen, together with the jewellery from the grave, at *L'Abbaye Notre-Dame* in *Châtillon-sur-Seine*.

The Merovingians quarried heavy stone and made sarcophaguses in which they buried their dead and placed them together, in parallel rows, in cemeteries. The sarcophaguses were often beautifully-carved if the person had been important, or made from simple plain slabs of solid stone for lesser mortals. In *Avallonnais* there are sarcophagus quarries, and towns such as *Quarré-les-Tombes* which specialised in their fabrication.

Close to *Camp Cora* on the *Via Agrippa* there is a Merovingian Sarcophagus quarry. If you take the walk along the meander of the River *Cure* towards *St. Moré* from the *Grottes d'Arcy*, there is a pathway signposted '*La Roche Taillée*' rising steeply up the cliff to your right. Follow these signs and after about three kilometres you will come to a quarry in the side of a solid cliff-face. It looks as if the workers decided to leave one day, downed-tools, and just walked off the job. There are half-quarried slabs, and work-in-progress. There's no explanation as to why there is this Mary Celeste feel about the place. In the 1930s a sculptor responded to the strange atmosphere by carving the head and torso of a wood nymph out of a piece of fallen rock. You have to look carefully to see it. Another quarry is to be found at *Champ Retard* north of *Avallon*. From the quarries, the stone was transported via the River Cure and along the *Via Agrippa* and other smaller roads to where it was going to be processed.

The town of *Quarré-les-Tombes* was one such centre for manufacture. It was linked to the Via Agrippa by the secondary roman road Julian l'Apostat, across the River *Cure* at *Les Fontaines Salées*. The road continued through the *Morvan* to the important Celtic oppidum of *Bibracte* on *Mount Beuvray*, which is now the site of the excellent Museum of the Celts. *Quarré-les-Tombes* is very interesting and ancient. In the fifth century it was known as '*Careacus in pago avalensis*'.[95]

Numerous finds have been reported over the years, including a statue of Mercury, ceramic tiles and mosaics, coins, and what is thought to be a statuette of Diana. A stone wayside marker is thought to represent Mars. Most of these were discovered out of the town centre, as it now is, in a place called *Les Boyes*, or *Champ Rouges*. The finds are exhibited in the *Saint-Père-sous-Vézelay* museum.

As an ancient and prominent town in the Morvan, *Quarré-les-Tombes* and its environs are rich in the three famous Morvan resources – two of them still in great demand today – water, wood and wet nurses. Given the topography, there is no reason to believe that these resources date only from the beginnings of written records. It is conceivable that the harvesting of wood has been carried on by logging and rafting down the water-courses to the more populous plains, and large cities, for centuries. Wet nurses would always be in great demand at a time when life and death were so determined by chance.

But the main reason why the town is known, is because of the many sarcophaguses – which can still be seen surrounding the *Eglise Saint-Georges*. In 1674 they numbered over 500 – fancifully, from time to time the number rose to 2000 – but there are far fewer now – many having been used for building or taken away for domestic/agricultural use. A local story tells of one furious priest of the town who destroyed many of the sarcophaguses himself to prevent his people stealing any more, and endangering their souls.

The legend connected with *Quarré-les-Tombes* and the sarcophaguses is about a battle against the '*Sarrasins*' – or about a battle against the '*Normans*' – The traditional site for the battle was *'la Chagnis'* or east of the town at places called *Champs Cullant* or *Champculan*. The battle of *Vaubeton* as described in *Girart de Roussillon,* has also been mentioned in connection with *Quarré-les-Tombes*. Whatever and wherever the battle, the story goes that thousands of good French soldiers were left for dead. So Saint George appeared and rained down the sarcophaguses from Heaven so that the men were able to be buried decently, thus securing his position as patron of the Church there, and providing the rest of us with a few anxieties about the health and safety aspects of his actions!

Somehow this story should be important to King Arthur's Burgundy. There is the obvious British connection with Saint George, but that was of course, much, much later. There's also the possibility that the battle of *Vaubeton* might have included the shadow of an ageing British knight called '*Drogon*'. But is there the smallest echo of Arthur's final battle against Mordred, named by Geoffrey as 'Camblan', in the place name of a possible *Quarré-les-Tombes* battle at **Champculan?** Camblan is not mentioned as one of Nennius' 'twelve battles', it is only mentioned in Geoffrey of Monmouth's **History.** If elements of the three fictional battles *Vaubeton, Champculan* and Camblan, are combined, together with the idea that the sarcophaguses were made for the purposes of mopping up the war-dead, then we could have found a new battle that was the basis for Geoffrey's account of Arthur's final conflict against Mordred/Morvandus/Arvandus.

It is generally believed that the town was a production centre for the sarcophaguses, and that they were stockpiled there until needed. It remains difficult to understand why the stones were transported such a long way from the quarries. It must have been hard work. Tough on the men – tough on the oxen. Were the masons of *Quarré-les-Tombes* more skilled than any working nearer? Was there some more mystical reason? It's one of those legends that meanders around without reaching any satisfying conclusion. Neither does it lend itself fully to flights of fancy. Certainly, sarcophaguses were being made in the fifth century, and if Arthur was buried in one, it could well have been made in *Quarré-les-Tombes*.

Modern-day *Quarré-les-Tombes* is a strange place. Some would say it has a dark side, despite its popularity. Today the village is one of the livewires of the *Morvan*. The Sunday morning markets – the annual Craft Fair and flea market – the music events – a couple of terrific restaurants – the bar with live bands – the chocolaterie ... But, is everything overshadowed by all those sarcophaguses around the church? They give the place a constant connection with the grave. A village with '*Tombes*' in the title will always possess that slight spookiness. There are the ghost stories too. There are sightings of silent warriors moving through the square, walking on a level below the present car park. Walking so that their knees appear just above ground... Then there's the hare that frequents the market place on nights when there's a full moon ...

But *Quarré-les-Tombes* doesn't have the monopoly on the fifth century death industry. In the following *Avallonnais* locations Merovingian sarcophaguses, tombs and skeletons have been discovered: *Arcy-sur-Cure, Asquins, Avallon, Blannay, Brosses, Châtel Censoir, Domecy-sur-le-Vault, Foissy les Vézelay, Girolles, Givry, Island, St. Moré, St. Père, Sermizelles, Vault-de-Lugny and Voutenay-sur-Cure*. Most of these sites are next to the rivers *Cousin, Cure* or *Yonne* – as one would expect. But the biggest and most interesting site was the necropolis discovered at *Asquins/Vaudonjon*, close to *Les Fontaines Salées*.[96]

The huge Merovingian cemetery at *Vaudonjon* has been the subject of several digs since the beginning of the 20th century. The area covered 2800 square metres and follows the line of the valley at *Cercueils* by the river *Cure*. Over five hundred and fifty tombs were discovered. They were dated according to the accompanying grave goods as between the fifth and eighth centuries AD – which is early enough to put them within Arthur's time-frame. More than 930 objects have been retrieved ranging from pots and vases, jewellery, buckles and weapons to metal *plaques* and stones bearing inscriptions. One such stone, now widely believed to be a hoax, bears the inscription: "VIRGINIVS/ILLOS TUOS MAXIMUS S/CONSTINVIS IMP ROM/AN 440"[97]

Unfortunately, no one has yet found a stone inscribed with 'Here lies Arthur, fabulous King of the Britons' marking a grave containing a richly-decorated Merovingian sarcophagus, fit for a king. But *Vaudonjon* would be one of the obvious places to put him, if he'd died at *Les Fontaines Salées*.

ESCOLIVES-SAINTE-CAMILLE

The Merovingian burial site still evident, that has been the most developed in the area, is at *Escolives-Sainte-Camille*. It is about 10 kilometres south of *Auxerre*. It's a very important site – which is why everything's a bit more organised than usual. This only means that you have to explore by going on a guided tour – which happens on the hour, every hour, morning and afternoon during the tourist season. But don't forget the two-hour lunch break. You're taken to see the (under cover) Roman bath excavations and some really good finds in a large barn-like museum. I arrived on a bicycle and was rather awed to find myself the only visitor for the tour. The young man who was to take me round, eyed me nervously. I explained that I was looking for King Arthur, which did nothing to put him at his ease.

Escolives was discovered in 1955 when someone was digging up an ancient walnut tree and found several old tomb fragments lodged in amongst the roots. Further investigation led to the discovery of a full-scale Merovingian burial ground containing over 300 graves – so far. The site was so interesting that they kept on digging and layer by layer discovered a very well-preserved Roman thermal bath site and evidence of a Roman shrine to Mercury dating back to the second century. Mercury is a slippery customer. He has a long association with the arts, money-making and well-being – remits which don't necessarily sit happily together. They also found some other strange items such as leather shoes, which were preserved thanks to the humidity in the soil. In the museum you can see even older finds. Neolithic fragments of pottery and bronze. One is left wondering whether the skeleton in the Merovingian sarcophagus is real. I thought better of asking my guide if he knew who it was.

A last word on sarcophaguses. In one of the accounts of Arthur's exhumation at Glastonbury, Ralph of Coggeshall reported that King Arthur's body was found in 'a very old coffin'. Some translators take that to mean 'a very old sarcophagus'. Could he have been discovered in a full stone sarcophagus? All translations confirm the large stone slab to which the famous lead cross is attached. Could that stone slab have been of Merovingian origin, quarried and made in abundance around *Avallon?* And could his body, therefore, have been transported across Gaul and back to the west of England, much later, to be received and buried by the monks of Glastonbury?

THE JOURNEY HOME

According to Ralph the phrase on the lead cross says, *"Here lies the famous King Arturius, buried in the Isle of Avalon".* That seems fairly straightforward – but it doesn't actually *say* that where the body has been discovered *is* the Isle of Avalon. It says that the body was *buried there.* Ralph and other eyewitnesses go to almost ridiculous lengths to convince us that the Isle of Avalon *is* Glastonbury, as we have already seen. But it could mean nothing of the sort. It could mean simply, that he *was* buried in the Isle of Avalon. He could have been removed to Glastonbury at a later date.

It was quite common for revered and holy bodies and body parts to be carted around in the Middle Ages – throughout Europe. Especially when the race for good pilgrimage relics was at its height. We have already mentioned St. Martin, St. Germanus and Mary Magdalene. In Britain the story of St. Cuthbert and his 'uncorrupted' corpse being taken all over the north of England is very familiar. It would not have been at all unusual for the remains of a great king to be similarly treated. But as with Mary Magdalene, the problems would have been distance and transportability. How feasible would it be to transport a body from *Avallon* – from *Les Fontaines Salées* – back to Glastonbury? Well, there's a challenge that someone might care to take up. I would imagine though, that like St. Martin, the stone sarcophagus would have been abandoned from the beginning, in favour of a wooden casket – perhaps with carrying handles as is suggested by the model of St. Martin's to be found in the *Obédiencérie* owned by the *Domaine Laroche* in *Chablis.* Perhaps the lead cross on its own as a kind of luggage label, would have been the only 'packaging' taken, and his skeleton simply shrouded and transported on a cart.

This might suggest that the lead cross had its origin in Burgundy – and was made later than the fifth century. The use of lead was common enough in the vicinity of *Avallon,* and we have already noted the many forges in the area. Lead artefacts have been discovered in *Quarré-les-Tombes* for example.[98] If the lead cross was made later to identify and accompany Arthur's body on its journey, then that would account for the anachronistic lettering style which is sometimes quoted as proof positive that the whole King-Arthur-buried-at-Glastonbury story is a fraud.

So, if this hypothesis can be followed through for a moment, we have to ask who might have moved him – and when? My personal theory is that it could have been journeymen masons. They had the strength, the freedom and the motivation.

In the 1180s there was a tremendous burst of religious building – both in Britain and in France. It was almost as if there was a competition to see who could build the richest and grandest churches, abbeys and cathedrals. In England, work had commenced on what was to be Wells Cathedral.

Glastonbury Abbey was being rebuilt after the fire in 1184. In France the Church of *St. Lazare* in *Avallon* had been started and so had the basilica at *Vézelay*. In 1166, Thomas Becket was in exile in *Vézelay* preaching against Henry II of England. After his return to England he was murdered in Canterbury Cathedral in 1170. Four years later, Canterbury Cathedral itself burned down, and the man employed to rebuild it was William of *Sens*. Communications between Burgundy and England were never better.

Over the next decade it was a good time to be a highly skilled and creative stonemason. It was a difficult time for Henry II, raising funds for Canterbury, and Glastonbury, and seeking atonement for the murder of Thomas Becket. It was therefore a good time to present the King of England with a highly prized, authenticated relic. A group of craftsmen bringing Arthur's body back from France sometime between, say, 1175 and 1185 would have been well-rewarded. Perhaps the King saw an opportunity to restore his royal credibility amongst his subjects. Perhaps he wanted recognition for his 'spiritual' nature – approbation for his piety from the church. Perhaps he saw the need to consolidate his kingdom and scotch for ever the rumour amongst the Welsh that Arthur would return 'from Avalon' to lead their nation. Any or all of those reasons could have led to a little conspiracy, and a secret re-burial of a body first buried in *Avallon*, Burgundy, and then subsequently and very publicly, exhumed in 1191. This would allow for the King to have pre-knowledge of the burial. But alas, Henry died in 1189. His errant son Richard came back to England for a whistlestop tour in order to raid the coffers to fund the Third Crusade he was about to undertake with his closest friend and ally, King *Phillippe* of France. He was not interested in Glastonbury. All building ceased on the new Abbey. Richard couldn't wait to get back across the Channel.

As a final comment about the feasibility of a return journey, in theory it would have been possible to transport the body from *Avallon* back to England, by water. The landing stage on the River *Cure* known since Roman times to have existed at *Gué Pavé* as part of the iron smelting and forging industry, and very close to *Les Fontaines Salées*, could have been the embarkation point. The route then would have followed the River *Cure* downstream, joining up with the River *Cousin* and quickly reaching the confluence with the River *Yonne* at *Cravant.* We know that much later, boat-building was one of the major cottage industries of *Sermizelles*. The River *Cure* must therefore have been navigable from there to Paris. Heading downstream, the *Yonne* passes through *Auxerre* and *Sens* meeting the River *Seine* just south of *Fontainbleau.* From there northwards to what is now *Le Havre* would have been part of a well-used river route into the English Channel. The beauty of using the rivers was that there was little possibility of getting lost. It would simply have been a question of letting the rivers carry you on downstream, with very little effort needed, until hitting the Channel coast. Safety from outlaws was another matter, however, and one would imagine that some care went into disguising the cargo.

THE CAVE IN THE HILLSIDE

There is an interesting variant of the Geoffrey of Monmouth version of King Arthur's death, probably written about a hundred years later – and possibly written to give us all a little more story to chew on than Geoffrey's brief account. The origins of the legend are unclear, but probably pre-existed in the oral tradition, which means that it might have some authenticity as an independent Arthurian source. The legend goes along these lines.

Arthur dies in 'The Island of Avalon' and his body is embalmed in balsam and myrrh, and placed in a coffin. It is taken to a little chapel. The door of the chapel is so narrow that people have to turn sideways to get through. It is too narrow for the coffin, which is left outside on a bier while the burial service is performed inside. A savage thunderstorm breaks over the chapel. The wind blows and there is an earthquake. A great mist descends and shrouds the bier from sight – lasting from morning until that afternoon. Finally, when the air clears, there is no trace of the coffin. The king had been taken to his final resting place, which appears to the onlookers to be a sealed, natural cave in the hillside.

The *Avallonnais* is pitted with limestone caves. One and a half million years ago a warm, shallow sea lapped around the southernmost parts of the Paris Basin. The coral reefs expanded thanks to trillions of tiny chalk-making creatures. When the sea finally retreated it left a *massif* of limestone which was shaped and eroded by the River *Cure* – flowing straight from the gravely granite heights of the *Morvan*. Where the river couldn't cut through – it went round. Thus the two giant meanders at *Arcy-sur-Cure* and *St. Moré* were formed. There was a third meander – but time and the river dislodged a giant rock, now called '*Rocher de la Vierge*', which fell in its path and made it change course. Over the millennia rain, slightly acidic with carbon dioxide, ate into the limestone and formed the important cave network. The resulting area is designated an Historical Monument and an Archaeological Site of National Interest.

There is a guided tour through the Great Cave of *Arcy*, or you can go on your own to explore the caves of *St. Moré* – this latter expedition being only for the truly intrepid, and sound of wind and limb. Whilst you're in *St. Moré* call in at the 'museum' which is in someone's barn. If you can raise anyone then ask to borrow the key to the church. Like most of the rural churches in Burgundy it could do with a few hundred thousand euros spending on it. But inside there's a beautifully carved Merovingian sarcophagus in the porch.

In the *Grottes d'Arcy* [caves at *Arcy-sur-Cure*] prepare to be astonished at the limestone rock formations. This is Wookey Hole, near Glastonbury, on a grand scale. You can be forgiven for believing at times that you are on a sci-fi film set. It seems improbable that such fantastic shapes and sculptures have been fashioned simply through the action of water on rock. The 'mites and 'tites transform caverns into weird rooms of cathedral proportions. It's no wonder that in our attempts to comprehend and order what we see, that we've given homely names to certain structures and formations. So we wander through *'La Salle de la Danse'* (The Dance Room), *'La Salle de la Draperie'* (The Room of Curtains), the *'La Salle des Vagues de la Mer'* (Sea Waves Room) and *'Lavoir des Fées'* (The Fairies' Wash House). There's a large pond in which an upside-down reflection of the cave above presents a plausible miniature world with a village, shoreline and crenellated castle. We can let our imaginations loose on the random shapes that seem to resonate with religious significance – *'Le Calvaire'* (the Calvaries), *'La Salle de la Vierge'* (Virgins with Child), *'Le*

Cierge Pascal' (the Paschal Candle) and of course, the *'La Coquille St. Jaques'* (Scallop Shell) – the familiar emblem of pilgrims on this ancient route to Compostella.

Some of the earliest art ever discovered has been found in the *Arcy* caves. The Horse Cave, which is not open to the public because of its inaccessibility and the vulnerability of the art work, contains engravings in a good state of preservation. There are bison, deer and abstract designs, and eight more or less complete mammoths. The Great Cave contains engravings and paintings of 20 mammoths (including a carved one), bears, oxen, horses, a rhinoceros, bison, a bird and a big cat and eight hand prints. There are also miscellaneous designs. As with all prehistoric art you need a good imagination. The guide will happily help you to look and see what's there. But the hand prints are quite distinctive. And eerie. What on earth was their purpose?

But much closer to *Les Fontaines Salées* is a cave that is hardly acknowledged outside the locality. At the top of the Scorpion hill, many meters underneath what's now the *Vézelay* basilica, lies a vast, natural cavern.

> *"Dans les petites falaises bordant la colline existe une vaste grotte dite de la Madeleine, qui n'a jamais fait l'objet d'aucune fouille."*[99]
> **[Translation: Amongst the small cliffs that border the hill there's a vast cave called *la Madeleine*, <u>which has never been the subject of an investigative dig</u>.]**

Of course I set out to find the cave, and stumbled clean over the Scorpion's vicious tail, and found instead an all-too-human tale. There is a cave up there, and it is privately owned, and not accessible to the public. I was not allowed to see it, to photograph it or to describe where it is. But I have seen some photographs. The colours of the dripping limestone marbled with mineral deposits and lichen were breathtaking. But, after comparing the size of what I saw in the photographs with the above description, I'm not entirely convinced that this is the right cave anyway. But it might be – if it went further back into the rock. For the time being it has to remain a mystery – and no, I couldn't see any skeletons. But, if I were a maverick archaeologist I'd be reaching for my trowel in the dead of night ……

8
AVALLON – THE END OF THE JOURNEY?

King Arthur and Arthur Riothamus merge in *Avallon*. And in *Avallon* their stories disappear. Whatever gallant quests, struggles, betrayals and fantasies were added in subsequent centuries, King Arthur's story always ends in 'Avalon'. Arthur Riothamus – the closest we're ever going to get to the 'real' King Arthur – disappears from history after he made his escape from *Bourges* to the *Burgundians*. There are two options in both cases. Either he died in *Avallon,* or he didn't. If he died in *Avallon* we've looked at a number of possible options as to what may have happened to him.

If Arthur didn't die straight away, or was cured of his wounds, then we have even greater scope for speculation. Let's imagine that he decided to stay in *Avallon.* Any soldier would be reluctant to return home as a defeated ex-hero. He might have preferred to remain in the country of his *'jeunesse'*. He could have converted to Christianity and joined a religious community at *Véziliacus* or in *Island* – by the lake on the Island of Willows. Perhaps he decided to continue to fight alongside the Franks against the Romans – and as a veteran soldier he took part in the Battle of Soissons. He could still have been alive by the time of the 'real' battle of *Soissons* in 486 AD. Perhaps he joined King *Clovis* there, to finally defeat the Romans led by Syagrius. That same Syagrius who had failed to keep his promise to Arthur of back-up troops in *Bourges.* Geoffrey of Monmouth may have got his history and geography a bit muddled. Was the Battle of *Soissons* the enigmatic battle which is variously transcribed as *Saussy, Siesa, Assnessia, Suesia* and *Soissie* in different manuscript versions of his **History**? And that battle which took place, according to Geoffrey, just outside *Autun,* could have been the Battle of 'Camblan' in Burgundy on the plains of Vaubeton at a place called *Champculan* giving us the root of the character 'Drogon' in the **Chanson de Geste de Girart de Roussillon.**

Inevitably the outcome of this research has raised more questions than it answers. It has also revealed a number of coincidences that are difficult to ignore. Coincidences that hop back and forth between the boundaries of fact and fiction.

These coincidences are about the geographical proximity of people, things and events. In *Avallonnais* for example we have the size, scope and reputation of the metal industries since Celtic times and the billeting of Sarmatian troops, known for their weapon-making, in *Sermizelles* – both 'facts'. We have Arthur's sword Caliburn forged in 'Avalon' and a character called 'Drogon' wearing a coat of mail made in 'the forges of Espandragon' – both fiction, but from different British and French literary traditions. Centuries later Richard Coeur de Lion is in *Vézelay* with Caliburn – 'fact'. What do these coincidences really mean? What course of events could have seen the survival and passing-on of Arthur's sword Caliburn, or Uther Pendragon's coat of mail? How did these objects come to be in *Avallon* and if they were brought there by Arthur, what happened to them after his death?

According to the new cultural industry that is Mary Magdalene, Arthur has swooped into the picture like a mighty dragon to reveal that he is, as well as everything else, of the Holy Bloodline and a direct descendant of Jesus. No matter how fantastical, unlikely and sensational, this is another coincidence of geographical proximity with *Avallon*. The cult of Mary Magdalene was founded in *Vézelay* with various myths about her travelling through France with her siblings and Joseph of Arimathea. Other myths relate to her relics – which are still to be found there in the crypt of the basilica – and which were 'rescued' from Provence and brought to *Vézelay* by *Bodilon* for *Girart de Roussillon*. These are the old stories, and there are many links, through time and place, between them and Glastonbury. The saints and hagiography surrounding Arthur in Britain also surround him in Burgundy, and in Brittany.

There are loose ends. For example, if Arthur's body was taken back to Glastonbury, who or what was Guinevere's skeleton that was found with it in the tomb when it was opened? Who is Arthur's 'second wife'? The chances of her being called 'Guinevere' too are pretty remote. And how did she get to share a tomb with him?

Geoffrey of Monmouth suggests that King Arthur had two campaigns in Gaul, and spent about 12 years there. This has provoked creative thinking about Arthur Riothamus, and the other occasions when he must have been in France. Riothamus undoubtedly knew his way around and probably knew the language as well. He was well-known to leading figures in Gaul – Aegidius, Sidonius, Syagrius. He knew Burgundy, and as its over-king, he knew Brittany too.

Riothamus' escape from *Bourges* and arrival in Burgundy cries out for narrative development.

In **History** Geoffrey paints a picture of King Arthur's court in England as being full of foreign dignitaries and V.I.P. visitors from overseas. We know that *Germanus* visited England twice, why not others? Invitations would have been reciprocated in Gaul. Later romance would have us believe that Arthur's court was cosmopolitan and alive with new ideas and fashions. Archaeology reveals widespread trading between Britain and Gaul in luxury goods such as wine, gold, silver, lead, tin, pottery and glass. A commercial and creative exchange between the two cultures would have existed alongside the military allegiances.

DIJON

Arthur Riothamus was not a typical uncouth warrior. Sidonius tells us that. I should like to believe that on his odyssey, he did more than simply trash everything that stood in his way. During those years in Gaul perhaps he spent some time admiring the cities, as well as 'subduing' them. Did he visit *Dijon,* and meet 'the blessed Gregory' – Gregory of Tours' great-grandfather. *Dijon* wasn't yet a city, but from this account by Gregory of Tours, it sounds charming:

> "There lived at that time in the city of Langres the blessed Gregory, a great bishop of God, renowned for his signs and miracles. And since we have spoken of this bishop, I think it not unpleasing to insert in this place an account of the site of Dijon, where he was especially active. It is a stronghold

with very solid walls, built in the midst of a plain, a very pleasant place, the lands rich and fruitful, so that when the fields are ploughed once the seed is sown and a great wealth of produce comes in due season. On the south it has the Ouche, a river very rich in fish, and from the north comes another little stream, which runs in at the gate and flows under a bridge and again passes out by another gate, flowing around the whole fortified place with its quiet waters, and turning with wonderful speed the mills before the gate. The four gates face the four regions of the universe, and thirty-three towers adorn the whole structure, and the wall is thirty feet high and fifteen feet thick, built of squared stones up to twenty feet, and above of small stone. And why it is not called a city I do not know. It has all around it abundant springs, and on the west are hills, very fertile and full of vineyards, which produce for the inhabitants such a noble Falernian that they disdain wine of Ascalon. The ancients say this place was built by the emperor Aurelian." [100]

I'm sure that Arthur would have spoken to great men and women, listened to their wisdom and admired their learning. With such a hands-on warrior style of living, he could not have had time to do much reading, or contemplation, himself. Perhaps he chose to spend the rest of his life in Burgundy studying at the great centres of learning, in *Auxerre, Autun* and *Sens.*

ALESIA

I'm also sure that Arthur Riothamus would have visited the site of *Alésia* – as a tourist. He'd have gone there to exercise his imagination. To put himself into *Vercingetorix's* sandals and gaze out onto Caesar's massed legions who were biding their time before their attack, in the famous siege of *Alésia*. There is a problem, though. I wonder which site his guide would have taken him to? There's the official site up on the hills collectively known as *Mont Auxois* – the one that has had all the investment and become an 'open archaeological park' as it says in the guidebook.

Then there's the undeveloped, unexcavated site up on *Montfault* and *La Montagne de Verre* (forgetting the modern-day quarry for the moment, which is even now blasting more metres off the top of the mountain for road-building). That's the one that *Bernard Fèvre* spent most of his life trying to convince everyone was the real *Alésia*. The powers that be have not yet been moved, though. I wonder if that has anything to do with the quarrying operation?

Then there's the *Montmarte/Sermizelles* theory. *(www.alesia-et-dependances.fr)* To say nothing of a few other sites around Gaul laying claim to it. Wherever it was, the familiar story is the same.

It's about the plucky Gauls coming together in 52 BC under *Vercingetorix*, to fight the mighty Julius Caesar and his Roman legions. They lost, of course, but not without years of causing Caesar plenty of grief. It was the final battle for Gaul, and thereafter Gaul became part of the Roman Empire. At the 'official site', *Vercingetorix* looms large over the little village of *Alise-Sainte-Reine*. He stands 46' high, fixing us with an impossibly romantic Gallic glare, and sporting exactly the kind of luxuriant moustache that prompted Ceasar's comment about the Celts being 'long-haireds'.

The day that I visited the site was in the middle of summer, and baking hot. There was no wind, and only a few other pink tourists struggling to cope with both the heat and with the plan of the site, trying to make sense of the piles of rubble and hillocks that are said to be the vestiges of the great oppidum – or fortress – where the Gauls holed-up. Customarily, when threatened, they would head for the high ground, inside the defensible walls, where the warriors would protect the community. I did as advised by the guidebook, and climbed up the little hill, the *'belvédère'*, to get a general view of the battle site. The book says, "You will then be in the same position as the Gauls, trapped in this oppidum with *Vercingetorix*, looking at the Roman troops gathered in the plains and on the hills." Certainly, for a young *Aeduen* girl being trapped anywhere with *Vercingetorix* would have had its appeal, but, I was not convinced. I looked out on the one side to the very steep hill I'd come up to get to the entrance and ticket office. Then I looked out across a vast plain in the other direction – stretching for miles into the distance, the grass rippling like an ocean as far as the eye could see. I suffered an imagination crash. I could not imagine anyone defending this site. Neither could I imagine that I was in a place of safety. It was wide open, exposed to the elements, and vulnerable. How could *Vercingetorix* and his men have built walls sufficient to enclose a plain? And why would they even have selected it when there must be sites far better suited, with more, natural defences, which would at least minimize the wall-building? The Gallo-Roman town built on top of the oppidum is very interesting, as is the little museum in *Alise-Sainte-Reine*. But I'm not persuaded that this site is *Alésia*. This is not the book to explore that controversy, but at risk of stating the obvious, there are parallels with Avalon and Glastonbury.

SOURCE OF THE SEINE

It is sometimes suggested that Arthur himself, as he becomes older, carries with him a strong sense of melancholy. In the stories that are subsequently written about him he often takes a lesser role than his 'knights', leaving the adventures and glory to them. His central and almost Greek tragedy, which is rarely exploited in modern interpretations, is that he failed to produce a legitimate heir. In Geoffrey of Monmouth's account he spent long periods of time away from Guinevere who ultimately betrayed him with the shadowy and evil Mordred. Literature would have us believe that not only was Morgen le Fay associated with Avalon, but that she could have been the reason why Arthur failed to return to Britain. Circumstantial evidence might also suggest that his lack of an heir became so important to him as he grew older that he travelled widely to visit a range of shrines in Burgundy known for their efficacy. Wace captures the sentiment:

"The sorer sorrow that he was a childless man."

Whether he was Christian or Pagan, the consequence of Arthur having no progeny was dire indeed. This could have preoccupied him for the rest of his years. The most efficacious shrine in Burgundy was to *Sequana* – the fertility goddess of the Source of the River *Seine*. Arthur would have been a pilgrim there.

The famous River *Seine* rises in relative obscurity today in north-east Burgundy. After following rusty signs through sparsely populated villages it is something of a surprise to arrive at an enclosure announcing that it is part of '*La Ville de Paris*' – and not part of the Department of the *Cote d'Or* at all. Like all the best sites, I find, it doesn't look promising to begin with. Go in through the gate. There is no charge.

After descending a little hill you will see a small garden shed. During the season, and possibly at weekends and on public holidays, it may be open. The shed houses a few postcards and plans of the site, and exhorts you, through a yellowing notice pinned inside the window, to visit the museum in *Dijon* which displays all the exciting finds resulting from excavations there. Follow the little stream up the valley. You come to a boggy pool then cross over a small stone bridge, and on a little further to the man-made 'grotto' (1868 – Napoleon III's orders) complete with reclining nymph put there by *Dijon* sculptor *Auban* in 1934. There was a previous nymph by *François Jouffroy*, apparently. No one seems to know what happened to her. It's now a modest little place, but things weren't always this low-key.

In Celtic times it was the site of the sacred pool of *Sequana* – the celebrated fertility and healing goddess of Burgundy. Once it was a major destination for a heaving mass of pilgrims, with all the paraphernalia that goes with them: hostelries; stalls selling votaries; food; wine; bathing houses and so on. The pilgrims come, full of hope, for a cure for their ailments or for those of their loved ones. We can only imagine the festivities, rites and rituals as the Celts wrote nothing down, but it has been possible to date the coins and little *ex votos* of stone and wood found in vast numbers (upwards of 1500) back to at least 150 BC – before the Roman conquest.

The ex votos have great charm as objets d'art. This is how they work. You placed a little effigy of the ailing part (an ear, foot, leg, lung, head etc. etc.) into the pool for *Sequana* to work her magic. They also tell the stories of the pilgrims – their health problems – and their offerings of thanks. Stone statuettes of children holding puppies or rabbits suggest that these might have been offerings of thanks. *Ex votos* of women with large bellies, or couples entwined together, or swaddled babies suggest *Sequana's* function as a fertility goddess. There are also faces, torsos and abstract sculptures whose meanings are not clear. The objects were found in the boggy pond which may once have been the ritual bathing pool. In the waterlogged earth the wooden sculptures were as well-preserved as the stone and bronze. In 1932 the famous bronze of *Sequana* herself – in a boat with a duck's head – was discovered by *Henry Corot*.

The *Sequana* finds are in the excellent *Musée Archéologique de Dijon*, but many fascinating ex votos discovered in other wells and springs in the *Châtillonais* can be seen at the museum in *Châtillon-sur-Seine* when you visit the amazing 'Treasure of Vix'. And of course, there's that dangling phallus from *Les Fontaines Salées* at *St. Père* museum…

The *Ville de Paris* knew what it was doing when it sequestered the three or four hectares surrounding *Sequana's* pool in 1867. How clever to have founded itself by a river with such auspicious beginnings.

It is unsatisfactory to leave things there. But the purpose of this research has only been to look at 'Avalon' in the light of the real *Avallon* in Burgundy, and its relevance to the King Arthur and Morgen le Fay of fiction, and the Arthur Riothamus of fact. In that respect, it's not easy to see any further ways forward other than to begin a new fiction about Arthur Riothamus and what happened to him when he reached *Avallon,* when the real history, as contained in the letters and the chronicles, stopped.

For now though, the concluding question has to be, has **'King Arthur's French Odyssey'** presented enough 'hazy memory' of King Arthur and Morgen le Fay in *Avallon* to excite the *Sociétié de Mythologie Française*?

Above all, has it allowed Arthur, fabulous King of the Britons, to take his rightful place in France, and to stride across the Burgundy landscape?

Northern and Central France, and South West England, showing the location of Burgundy.

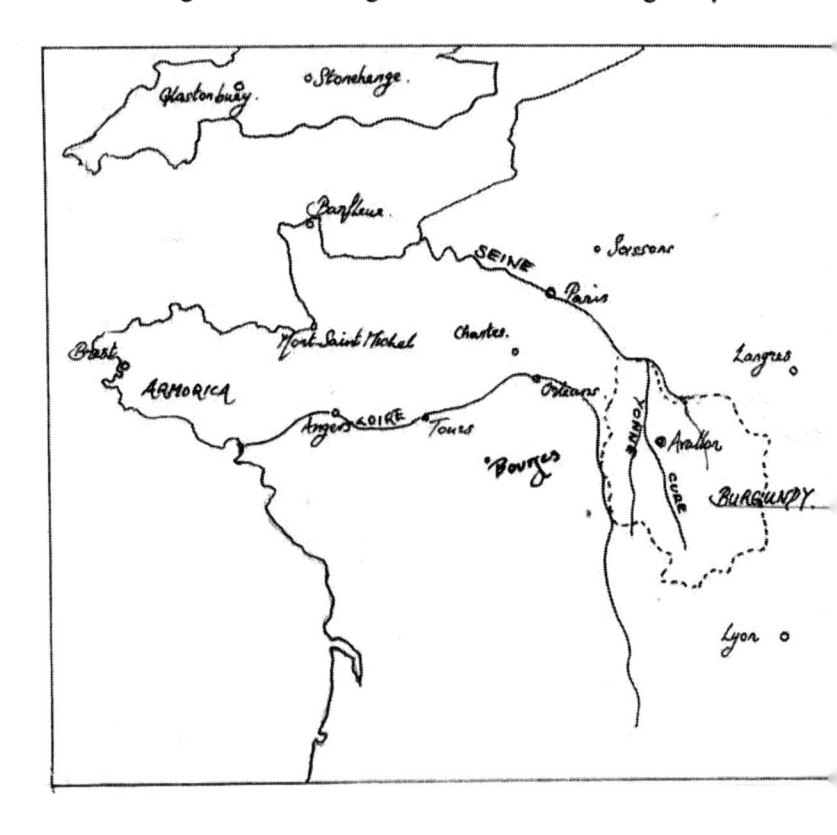

John Garlick

Burgundy

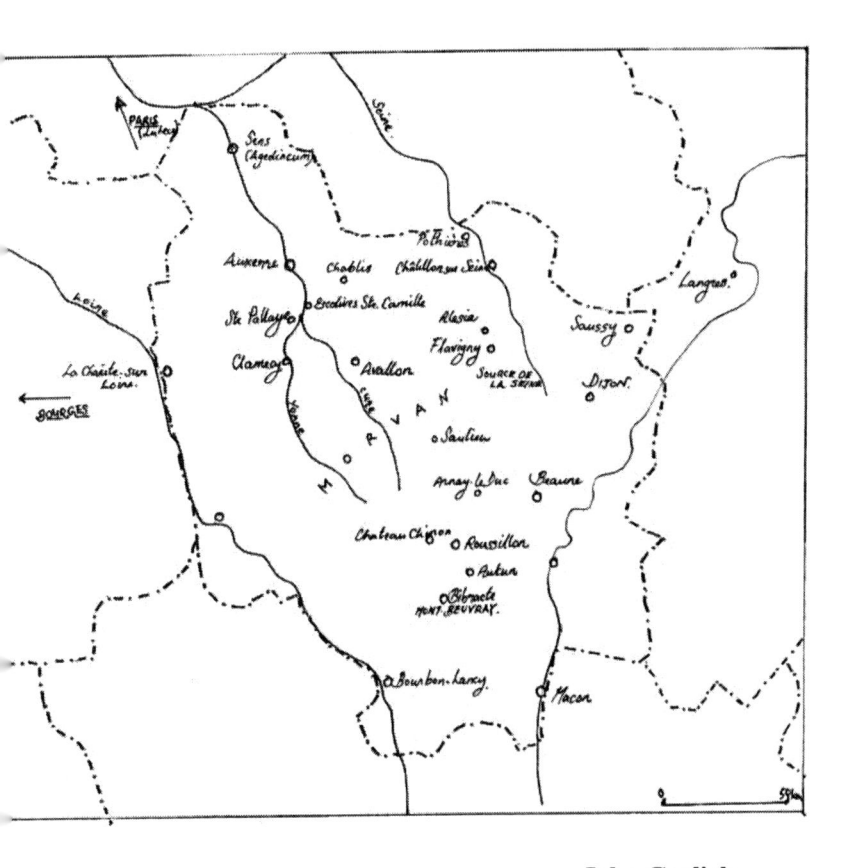

John Garlick

Avallonnais

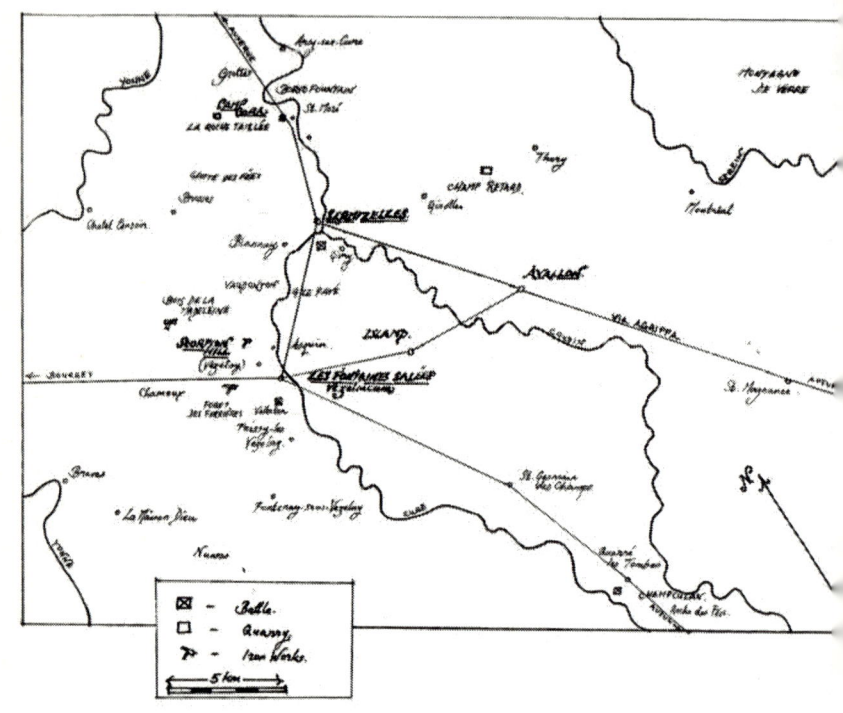

John Garlick

APPENDIX 1

Timeline

Most dates pre 12th century are open to interpretation. All dates mentioning King Arthur are conjecture.

PRE- Fifth CENTURY

316	St. Martin de Tours born
376	St Martin destroyed temple to Apollo in Avallon
378	St. Germanus born
390	St. Patrick born
391	Christianity became official religion of Roman Empire. Theodosius banned all pagan rites
395	Roman Empire split into East and West
396	Aëtius born
397	St. Martin de Tours died

Fifth CENTURY – ARTHUR'S CENTURY

400	Attila the Hun born
405	First Latin Bible translated from Hebrew by St. Jerome. Pelagius writing in Rome
407	Withdrawal of Roman troops from Britain. Constantine III, British Emperor goes to conquer Gaul
409	Germanus attends school in Avallon, Burgundy. Constans II becomes Emperor, Vandals and Alans overrun Spain

410	Visigoths sack Rome
411	Honorius tells Britons they must fend for themselves
418	Germanus elected Bishop of Auxerre. Pelagius declared heretic and banished. Visigoths moved into south-west Gaul and established their capital at Toulouse which was the first of the Germanic Kingdoms to be established. Ruled by Theodoric I
423	Honorius died
424	Aëtius leads an army of Goths and Huns to invade Rome
424	Valentinian III becomes Emperor of the West. Vortigern comes to power in Britain
426	Aëtius fights against the Goths and the Franks
430	Bishop Germanus of Auxerre and Bishop Lupus of Troyes go to Britain to preach against Pelagianism. Public debate at St. Albans. Whilst there Germanus sees active service against Saxons, the 'Hallelujah!' victory. Vortigern marries
431	Chlodio, first Frankish king, makes Tournai his capital. Aëtius drives back Franks. St. Augustine died
432	St Patrick made a Bishop at Auxerre then goes to Ireland and converts Irish to Christianity and established Irish Celtic Church. Sidonius born
433	Attila inherits Hunnish Kingdom
435	Burgundians attacked by Huns and then made peace with Aëtius. Aurelius Ambrosius succeeds as King of the Britons
436	Roman withdrawal from Britain complete. Gondioc succeeded Gundahar as King of Burgundians. Battle of Narbonne Aëtius defeats Visigoths
437	Uther Pendragon succeeds as King of Britons. Childeric I born

440	St. Leo I becomes Pope 'Leo the Great' 'The First Pope'
442	King Arthur born. Brilliant Comet VI seen for 100 days
446	'Groans of the Britons' – Saxons arrive in Britain in number under mythical leaders Hengist and Horsa
447	Germanus' second visit to Britain. Earthquake and eclipse of the sun.
448	Germanus died. Meroveus, first Merovingian Frankish King aged 15, succeeded Chlodio
449	Angles, Saxons, Jutes invade Britain. Britons flee in large number to Brittany. Vortigern invites Hengist and Horsa to Britain
451	Battle of Catalun Fields. Attila finally repulsed from Gaul by Aëtius. Merovingian dynasty established in Gaul. Haley's Comet lasted 68 days
452	Sidonius marries daughter of Avitus and moves to Clermont Ferrand. Attila turned back from Rome by Pope Leo
453	Attila died
454	Valentinian III murders Aëtuis.
455	Rome sacked by Vandals. Valentinian III murdered. Avitus becomes Western Roman Emperor. Saxons rebelled against Vortigern (last mention of Vortigern)
456	Meroveus died. Jutes invade Kent in Britain, invited by Vortigern. Rome in chaos
457	Arthur succeeded to throne. Beginning of Domestic Campaign. Childeric I became second Merovingian King of Franks. Leo I becomes Roman Emperor
461	St. Patrick died. Pope St. Leo died. Hilarus became Pope. Lyon became new capital of Burgundians

463	With Aegidius, Childeric I fought the Visigoths in Angers and Orleans. Was Riothamus there? Gunderic died. Gundobad took title of King of Burgundians
464	Aegidius died. Arvandus (Morvandus), Prefect, is exiled by Rome for treason
466	Euric becomes King of Visigoths – conquers Marseilles. Clovis born
468	Sidonius describes life in Rome. Syagrius, son of Aegidius, succeeds
469	Riothamus goes to Gaul
470	Riothamus disappears from Bourges – heading towards the Burgundians. Last mention of Riothamus. Sidonius becomes Bishop of Clermont Ferrand
472	Vesuvius erupts – ash was experienced in Constantinople
473	Gundobad died
475	Sidonius imprisoned by Visigoths. Cadbury Castle in England (Camelot) re-occupied. Ambrosius drove Saxons back to Isle of Thanet
476	Western Roman Empire comes to an end
477	Saxons arriving in Britain
480	Constantinople earthquake – 40 days
481	Clovis I becomes third Merovingian King of the Franks aged 15, considered to be the first 'French King'
486	Battle of Soissons – Syagrius v. Clovis. Clovis defeated Syrigius and what was considered the last bit of Roman land in Gaul was gone. Was King Arthur there?

493	Clovis converts to Christianity and is baptised and forces his troops to do likewise. Clovis m. Clothilde, a Burgundian Princess
494	Gildas born. Battle of Mount Baden British against Saxons. Arthur's Men?
495	Saxon Cerdic lands in Dorset, England
500	Clovis defeats Burgundians at Dijon
507	Clovis defeats Visigoths with help of Burgundians at the battle of Vouillé. Makes his new base in Paris
511	Clovis died buried on south bank of Seine in Paris
534	Franks conquered Burgundians
538	Gregory of Tours b. Author of **Historum Francorum**
546	Gildas wrote **de Excidio**
551	Jordanes wrote **Gothic History**
560	Gildas died
570	Prophet Mohammed born

THE RISE OF VÉZELAY, BURGUNDY

830	Nennius wrote **Historia Brittonum**. First mention of 'Villam Vizeliacum'
858	Founding of the monastery for women beside the River Cure (Les Fontaines Salées) by Girart and Berthe de Roussillon and their daughter Eva
877	Approval given by Pope John VIII that monastery could convert to house for men
887	Veziliacum and monastery beside Cure destroyed. Monastery 'moved' to top of Scorpion hill
900	Fire destroyed Veziliacum

1050   Mary Magdalene's bones in Vézelay verified by Pope Léon XI. Cult of Mary Magdalene established at Vézelay

TWELFTH CENTURY – THE STORY GOES ON

1100   Geoffrey of Monmouth born
1125   Glastonbury Abbey – Cloisters, Bell Tower, Chapter House, Refectory built
1136   **History of the Kings of Britain,** Geoffrey of Monmouth
1138   Beginning of the construction of the Romanesque basilica at Vézelay
1146   St. Bernard preaches the second Crusade at Vézelay
1150   **Chanson de Geste de Girart de Roussillon**
1152   **Vita Merlini,** Geoffrey of Monmouth. Henry Plantagenet marries Eleanor of Aquitaine
1154   King Henry II of England, reign begins
1155   Geoffrey of Monmouth died. **Roman de Brut,** Wace
1165   Hughes de Poitiers wrote the **Chronicles de Vézelay**
1166   Thomas Becket preaches against King Henry II of England at Vézelay
1170   Thomas Becket murdered in Canterbury Cathedral. **Eric and Enide,** Chrétien de Troyes
1174   Canterbury Cathedral burned down. William of Sens (Burgundy) hired to rebuild it.
1180   Wells in Somerset, England, Cathedral begun to be built
1184   Glastonbury Abbey, great fire destroys Abbey
1185   Choir & Gothic Transept at Vézelay begun to be built. **Perceval,** Robert de Boron

1186	King Henry II puts Ralph Fitzstephen in charge of re-building Glastonbury Abbey. St. Mary's Chapel rebuilt
1189	King Henry II died. Richard Coeur de Lion becomes King of England
1190	Third Crusade begins at Vézelay. Richard Coeur de Lion is in possession of Caliburn, King Arthur's sword
1191	King Arthur and his 'second wife', Guinevere, exhumed at Glastonbury
1199	Richard Coeur de Lion died

APPENDIX 2

HISTORICAL BACKGROUND NOTES

These notes are to aid the imagination, to help set the scene for King Arthur in France and to establish a sense of time and place, in what might be unfamiliar territory.

France was known as *Gallia* by the Romans, and its people as *Galli* – the Gauls. The Greeks knew them as *Keltoi* – which is where the word 'Celts' comes from. It's the Celts who have been credited with the 'civilisation' and the Gauls credited as the natives of what was then Gaul and is now France. In reality they were one and the same.

A simple history of France up to the fifth century can be divided into Pre-History, Celts/Gauls and Gallo-Romans. Each of these eras was influenced irrevocably by assorted invading 'barbarians': Franks, Goths, Vandals, Huns, Visigoths, Burgundians, Alans, etc. But the 'Celts' would not have recognised themselves as such – neither would the transitional 'Gallo-Romans'. And they certainly wouldn't have recognised that they were all slipping into something now referred to as 'The Night of the Merovingians' or in England, 'The Dark Ages'. One thing becomes another gradually, over a long period of time.

PRE-HISTORY

There has been a continuous human presence in Gaul since pre-historic times. In Burgundy the caves at Arcy-sur-Cure bear witness to all stages in human development from Neanderthal to Homo Sapiens.

Gaul was a vast area stretching from the Alps to the Pyrenees, and taking in all of modern-day France, Belgium, Luxembourg and most of Switzerland. The peoples were the result of continuous migration. There was a bewildering number of ethnic groupings. The world outside the tribal boundaries was shaped by travellers' tales and traders – and by encounters with other tribes – hostile and peaceful.

Some tribes had a profound influence on progress. Neolithic tribes from Provence spread north and west through Gaul and into Britain and brought a sophisticated ceramics industry and a belief-system centred on megaliths, tumuli and dolmen tombs. They understood astronomy. The stones and megaliths in Brittany at Carnac, and at Stonehenge in England date from these times.

Tribes from the Danube moved west. They brought with them the technology and expertise to build wooden houses in village groups. They brought livestock, cleared forests and planted cereal crops. These and other influences permeated Gaul, and the waves of settlers (or were they 'invaders'?) continued enriching and advancing the culture. Certain groups from what is now Switzerland, which would become known as the Celts, had a lasting effect on the whole of the Western world.

THE LEGACY OF THE CELTS

Geoffrey of Monmouth's King Arthur is neither Roman nor Anglo-Saxon. He represents an old Britain that existed before the Roman invasion – the Celts – the civilisation that originally came from Gaul. His greatest enemies were the Saxons, Picts and Scots, and, in Geoffrey's story, the Romans. To understand Arthur and his relationship with Gaul, it is necessary to understand his roots in Celtic culture.

The Celts are important to our story because their culture is at the heart of Arthurian legend. To this day, Brittany, Cornwall, Wales, Ireland and Scotland still claim a Celtic affinity with each other, dating back over two thousand years. Fierce nationalistic passions can still be roused by Celtic music and words. There are freedom warriors who still celebrate pre-Anglo-Saxon times and the supremacy of the Druids. There may even be some who are waiting for Arthur to turn up again, take hold of the reins and sort out a world that still needs its heroes. We find Arthur embedded in the Celtic stories of Wales passed down by oral tradition, written down centuries later. We find him in the Celtic legends and the place names of Brittany, Cornwall and Scotland. We find him in the genealogy of Irish warriors. These nations, pushed to their western limits, remain the guardians of Arthurian tradition. They are what is left of a way of life which began in continental Europe around 700 BC. This culture eventually gave way to aggressive invasion by the Romans, Angles, Saxons, Vikings, Normans and was changed for ever.

The Celts organised themselves through necessity into a competitive and hierarchical society. There were warrior chiefs and a warrior class, artisans, farmers, poets and musicians, and Druids. Unlike Roman women, Celtic women commanded respect and had a strong influence on public matters. They fought beside their husbands, and some achieved a high status in their own birthright or through their own abilities. The chief also had a band of personal followers; the Romans called them 'clients', who owed him allegiance in return for giving them his protection. When they were not in battle, the men wore woven woollen, plaid trousers. Julius Caesar called them 'trousered long-haireds' because they grew moustaches and kept their hair longer than the Romans.

The picture of the Celts as a strong, productive and artistically driven civilisation, listening to their long-haired bards making music in the twilight, enjoying plentiful food, fine Italian wine and wearing beautiful woven garments and golden torcs round their necks, has a New Age feel to it. But the Celts were not a gentle, peace-loving people.

Classical authors frequently refer to the Celts as quarrelsome and headstrong. In addition to their metal-working skills, the Celts are best remembered for their warlike dispositions and how both men and women went into battle wearing little but woad. They decapitated their foes, prizing their heads as trophies. They fought as mercenaries, and they also raided neighbouring tribes. Their favoured spoils of war were prisoners – men, women and children – which they enslaved either for their own purposes or for trading with the Etruscans for wine – of which they were extremely fond.

According to classical writers the ideal Celtic physical type was tall, muscular and blond. There is evidence to suggest they dyed their hair with lime-wash. As well as looking outrageous when they went to war, they also struck fear into the hearts of their enemies by the sheer noise they made. They used terrifying war cries and blew loudly on their famous trumpets before charging into battle in their two-wheeled chariots. In 225 BC Polybius writes that there was *"such a tumult of sound that it seemed that not only the trumpets and the soldiers but all the country around had got a voice and caught up the cry."* They were known to practise human sacrifice – and possibly cannibalism.

The Celts' religious leaders were the infamous Druids. They were an itinerant and executive class wandering from tribe to tribe not only presiding over religious ceremony but also dispensing justice. We know about them through Caesar's writings. They were a powerful force to be reckoned with. Their wisdom and counsel were highly prized. They inhabited a world of sacred oak and ash groves – mistletoe and magic – blood and sacrifice. Neither they, nor the musicians and bards who kept and told the stories of the tribe, took part in the warriors' contests or battles, or in the daily workloads of the artisans or farmers.

This deeply religious and bellicose country of poets, warriors and craftsmen was what greeted Julius Caesar when he arrived in Gaul in 58 BC. He had a struggle on his hands. The Celts were resilient and put up a strong fight. Although scattered and answering to many kings and chieftains, they united under their one great leader, Vercingetorix.

One of the most important Celtic tribes was the 'Aeduen' whose power-base covered much of present-day Burgundy, and from whose ranks emerged the mighty Vercingetorix who proved a thorn in Caesar's side for so many years. The Aeduen would have counted the town of Avallon as one of their major centres. Until his ultimate defeat and surrender at Alésia, Vercingetorix rallied disparate tribal groups against the Romans in a way that had never been achieved before. He is recognised now as the quintessential Gallic braveheart. As a force against Caesar he would have been an ancient hero for Geoffrey of Monmouth's King Arthur and his army, which came from all over Gaul as well as from Britain and Brittany.

After the defeat of Vercingetorix at Alesia, Gaul became a province of Rome.

GAUL UNDER THE ROMANS

The Gauls thrived under The Romans. As in Britain, the material benefits to the whole country were of course, immeasurable. The Romans were experienced invaders. Immediately following the invasion, and in one fell swoop, the Romans enlisted gangs of the most warlike Gallic youth and led them off for a tour of duty in foreign parts. They ennobled seasoned Celtic warriors as Roman commanders, paid and fed them well, gave them a powerful uniform, and offered them citizenship and new towns with modern facilities and amenities when they returned. The famous example being the Aeduen tribe's wholesale removal from their Celtic oppidum Bibracte, to the new, purpose-built city of Augustodonum (Autun). When it was built, Autun was said to rival Rome. In Geoffrey's '*History*' Arthur's second campaign in Gaul centres on Autun.

In addition to all the physical changes brought about by the Romans in Gaul, the abiding and significant cultural changes were the adoption of Latin as the basis for a vernacular French language, and the eventual introduction of a Rome-centred Christianity.

Celtic gods and their holy places were gradually taken over by the Romans and re-labelled according to their Roman gods. Then Christianity came along and did much the same again. But the transitions were not instantaneous. Beliefs merged and resisted sudden change. There must have been times when deities belonging to a number of religions existed side-by-side. It is not known how much of Gaul had been converted by the fifth century, except that Clovis 1st, known subsequently as the first King of France, did not convert until 493 AD. What all this means is that the starting point of a journey into even the most distant pagan past can sometimes begin at a site of saintly veneration or strong, present-day Christian significance.

By the fifth century Gaul was a bubbling melting pot containing the potential for some of the greatest changes and developments to affect western civilisation.
The end of the Roman Empire saw the rise of the Franks and the Merovingian dynasty, which under King Clovis I was to establish 'France'.

BIBLIOGRAPHY

Académie des Inscriptions et Belles-Lettres, Ministère de la Culture et de la Francophone *Carte Archeologique de la Gaule Pre-inventaire archéologique publié sous la responsabilité de* Michel Provost 6 Vols. (France from 1993)

Alcock, Leslie *Arthur's Britain* (Penguin Classic History, Penguin Books England 1971)

Anon. *La Chanson de Girart de Roussillon* (Trans. Micheline de Combarieu du Grès et Gérard Gouiran, Lettres Gothiques Livre de Poche Paris 1993)

Ashe, Geoffrey *Merlin – The Prophet and his History* (Sutton Publishing Gloucestershire England 2006)

Ashe, Geoffrey *The Discovery of King Arthur* (Sutton Publishing Gloucestershire England 2005)

Aubert, O. *Celtic Legends of Brittany* (Coop Breizh France 1993)

Auclerc, Robert *Mémoire en Images Avallon* (2 Vols. Alan Sutton France 2007)

Bonnet, Jacques *Le Site Sacré de Vézelay* (Editions J. Bonnet 42300 Roanne)

Boron, Robert de *Merlin and the Grail Josepf of Arimathea, Merlin, Percival* (Trans. Nigel Bryant. D.S.Brewer Cambridge 2007)

Boussel, Patrick *Guide de la Bourgogne et du Lyonnais Mystérieux* (Les Guides Noirs Editions Tchou Princesse France 1978)

Braudel, Fernand *The Mediterranean in the Ancient World* (Trans. Sian Reynolds, Allen Lane The Penguin Press London 2001)

Burgess, Glyn S., and Brook, Leslie C. *French Arthurian Literature Volume IV Eleven Old French Narrative Lays* (D.S. Brewer, Cambridge 2007)

Deyts, Simone *Un Peuple de Pelerins – Offrandes de Pierre et de Bronze des Sources de la Seine* (Revue Archeologique de l'Est et du Centre-Est, Dijon France 1994)

Eschenbach, Wolfram von *Parzival* (Trans. A.T.Hatto, Penguin Books London 1980)

Fevre, Bernard *Complexe du Siege d'Alesia en Terre-Plaine (*S.E.G.A.M.M. Association Alexandre Parat 1997)

Fortune, Dion *Glastonbury – Avalon of the Heart* (Weiser Books, USA 2000)

France, Marie de *The Lais of Marie de France* (Trans. Robert Hanning & Joan Ferrante A Labyrinth Book Baker Academic USA 2006)
Frizot, Julien *Vézelay* (Editions Gaud France 2002)

Geoffrey of Monmouth *The History of the Kings of Britain* (Trans. Lewis Thorpe Penguin Books London, 1966)

Green, Miranda J. *Dictionary of Celtic Myth and Legend* (Thames and Hudson London 1997)

Haase, Pierre *Le Canton de Vézelay "A La Belle Epoque"* (CIDAC Avallon 1986)

Haase, Pierre *Les Communes Rurales du Canton d'Avallon* (CIDAC Avallon 1987)

Hawkins, Desmond *Avalon and Sedgemoor* (Tabb House, Cornwall England 1989)

Heurley, A. *Avallon Ancien et Moderne* (Reprint of 1880 edition Librarie Voillot Avallon 1989)

Howard-Gordon, Frances *Glastonbury Maker of Myths* (Gothic Image Publications England 1982)

Kendrick, T.D. *The Druids* (Senate Studio Editions London 1994)

Lacroix, Bernard *Saint-Père-sous-Vézelay origins et évolution d'un village d'après les découvertes archéologiques* (Reprint from 1962, Librarie Voillot Avallon 1993)

La Varende, Gabriel de *Une Demeure Alchimique Le Château du Chastenay* (Editions du Chastenay, France 1990)

Lacy, Norris J., Ashe, Geoffrey with Mancoff, Debra N. *The Arthurian Handbook* (Second Edition Garland Publishing New York & London 1997)

Matthews, John *The Elements of the Arthurian Tradition* (Element Books Ltd. England 1989)

Meuleau, Maurice *Les Celtes en Europe* (Editions Ouest-France 2004)

Michell, John *New Light on the Ancient Mystery of Glastonbury* (Gothic Image Publications, Glastonbury England 1990)

Norton-Taylor, Duncan *The Celts* (Time Life International United States 1975)

Parc Naturel Regional MORVAN (Guides Gallimard Paris)

Petit, Ernest *Avallon et l'Avallonnais* (Reprint from 1867, Librarie Voillot, Avallon 1992)

Petit, Victor *Description des Villes et Campagnes du Departement de l'Yonne, Arrondissement d'Avallon* (Reprint from 1870, Librarie Voillot, Avallon 2001
Piggott, Stuart,. Daniel, Glyn and McBurney Charles *France Before the Romans* (Thames and Hudson London 1973)

Pujo, Bernard *Histoire de Vézelay* (Perrin France 2000)

Riguet, Georges *Contes Morvandiaux* (Editions Hérode France 2002)

Reid, Howard *Arthur the Dragon King The Barbaric Roots of Britain's Greatest Legend* (Headline Book Publishing London 2001)

Renaud, Guy *L'Aventure du Fer en Bourgogne de Bibracte au Creusot* (Alan Sutton Gloucestershire, England 2007)

Reno, Frank D. *Historic Figures of the Arthurian Era* (McFarland & Company America and London 2000)

Roy, Jules *Vézelay A Sentimental Journey* (L'Or des Etoiles 1995, 2004)

Sommet, M. *Topographie, Statistique, Histoire de la Ville de Vézelay* (Reprint from 1879 Librarie Le Bleu du Ciel, Vézelay 1990)

Scott, John and Ward, John O. *Hugh of Poitiers The Vézelay Chronicle* (Medieval & Renaissance Texts and Studies New York 1992)

Taverdat, Gérard *Noms de Lieux de Bourgogne* (Editions Bonneton Paris 1994)

Troyes, Chrétien de *Arthurian Romances* (Trans. William W. Kibler & Carleton W. Carroll Penguin Classics London 1991)

Vasseur, Guy *Les Carrières de Pierre du Nord-Est Avallonnais* (Guy Vasseur France 2008)

Vogade, François *Les Fontaines Salées* (Magasin St-Bernard Vézelay 1980)

Vogade, François *Vézelay – Symbolisme et Esotérisme* (Guillaudot France 1998)

Wace & Layamon *Arthurian Chronicles Roman de Brut* (Trans. Eugene Mason Kessinger Publishing USA)

MAPS
2722ET; 27220; 27210; 2721E; 28220T Cartes de Randonnées 1: 25 000 (Institut Geographique National)

MAGAZINES
Vents du Morvan (Spring/Summer 2000)
Bourgogne Spécial Celtes (November 2002), *Bourgogne* (15 February – 15 April 2005)
National Geographic France (April 2006)

INDEX

Aballo, 52, 127
Abbey, 16, 47, 55, 58, 61, 73, 87, 112, 134, 141, 143, 167, 168, 192, 193
Abbey Pierre-qui-Vire, 143
Adam of Domerham, 58
Aeduans, 129
Aegidius, 36, 44, 68, 149, 175, 190
Aëtius, 43, 44, 131, 187, 188, 189
Aignan of Orleans, 131
Alans, 43, 105, 187, 194
Alésia, 49, 50, 78, 79, 102, 107, 126, 139, 178, 180, 199
Andoche, 143
Aquitaine, 29, 40, 60, 192
Arcturus, 143, 144
Arcy-sur-Cure, 136, 162, 169, 170, 195
Armançon, 89
Armorica, 39, 97
Arnay-le-Duc, 143
Arvandus, 38, 78, 150, 161, 190
Ashe, Geoffrey, 201, 204
Asquins, 23, 83, 114, 130, 162
Association Alexandre Parat, 139, 202
Attila the Hun, 187
Aube, 147, 148
Autun (Augustodonum), 50
Auxerre (Autessiodurum), 68, 131
Avaleum, 53
Avalon, 11, 15, 17, 18, 19, 20, 25, 29, 31, 32, 33, 34, 46, 47, 48, 52, 53, 54, 55, 56, 57, 58, 59, 60, 61, 62, 63, 64, 65, 66, 72, 75, 96, 107, 117, 140, 151, 156, 165, 167, 169, 173, 174, 180, 183, 202, 203, 214
Avalonia, 53
Barfleur, 30, 147, 148
Barinthus, 32, 76
Beaune, 143
Bede, 21
Bibracte, 143, 145, 159, 199, 205
Blannay, 162
Bois-de-la-Madeleine, 100
Bonnet, Jacques, 201

Boulogne, 41, 50, 104
Bourbon-Lancy, 123
Bourg-de-Déols, 37
Bourges (Avaricum), 67
Brest, 32
Brèves, 102
Brigit, 61
Brittany, 21, 23, 28, 29, 35, 39, 97, 129, 131, 154, 175, 189, 195, 196, 199, 201
Brosses, 79, 162
Burgundians, 23, 35, 37, 43, 44, 48, 67, 99, 150, 173, 188, 189, 190, 191, 194
Caen, 64
Camelot, 46, 56, 57, 190
Camelot Project, 56, 57
Canterbury Cathedral, 167, 192
Chablis, 11, 130, 166
Châlon-sur-Saône, 143
Chamoux, 100
Chapelle du Saulce, 155, 157
Charité-sur-Loire, 38
Charlemagne, 23, 82
Charost, 38
Chartres, 32, 144
Châtel Censoir, 162
Châtel Gérard, 124
Châtillon-sur-Seine, 84, 87, 158, 182
Chrétien de Troyes, 22, 39, 63, 75, 192
Clamecy, 155
Clovis, 36, 45, 72, 149, 173, 190, 191, 200
Cocquilles St. Jacques, 115
Cocteau, 20
Constantine, 40, 72, 97, 187
Constantius of Lyon, 130
Cousin, 50, 51, 64, 86, 102, 103, 113, 124, 125, 154, 162, 168
Cravant, 168
Cro Magnon, 49
Crot de Tarnasse, 70
Crot-au-Port, 101
Cuthbert, 165
De Excidio Britanniae, 21, 40

Dijon, 124, 136, 143, 176, 181, 182, 191, 202
Domecy-sur-le-Vault, 162
Drogon, 84, 85, 86, 93, 94, 95, 96, 99, 107, 161, 174
Druids, 90, 126, 127, 128, 133, 196, 197, 198, 203
Dunstan, 61
Dux Bellorum, 21
Eglise Saint-Georges, 160
Eleanor of Aquitaine, 60, 192
Erec and Enide, 63
Escollives-Sainte-Camille, 132
Foissy-le-Vézelay, 91
Fontainbleau, 168
Fontaines Salées, 24, 50, 67, 68, 69, 70, 71, 72, 73, 74, 80, 81, 85, 86, 87, 89, 90, 91, 101, 102, 103, 115, 123, 126, 133, 141, 142, 148, 152, 155, 159, 163, 165, 168, 171, 182, 191, 205
Fontenay-près-Vézelay, 100, 101, 123
Fortune, Dion, 202
Franks, 35, 36, 37, 43, 44, 45, 149, 150, 173, 188, 189, 190, 191, 194, 200
Frollo, 29, 108
Gascony, 29
Gênes, 111
Geneviève of Paris, 131
Geoffrey of Monmouth, 16, 19, 20, 21, 23, 27, 30, 33, 35, 39, 41, 46, 47, 48, 50, 56, 60, 61, 62, 67, 72, 74, 76, 77, 81, 83, 96, 97, 98, 107, 108, 116, 120, 143, 145, 147, 161, 168, 173, 175, 180, 192, 196, 199, 203, 214
Germany, 44
Gildas, 21, 39, 43, 61, 191
Girolles, 123, 162
Givry, 86, 123, 162
Glastonbury, 16, 25, 26, 33, 46, 47, 50, 53, 55, 56, 57, 59, 60, 61, 62, 75, 76, 109, 113, 114, 116, 132, 134, 135, 138, 139, 140, 141, 142, 164, 165, 166, 167, 170, 175, 180, 192, 193, 202, 203, 204
Godegisel, 75
Godomar, 75
Gregory of Tours, History of the Franks, 37
Grotte des Fées, 79
Grottes d'Arcy, 123, 159, 170
Gué de Saint-Jean, 153
Gué Pavé, 100, 168

Guinevere, 25, 29, 30, 33, 55, 56, 59, 75, 132, 175, 180, 193
Guingamar, 63, 75
Gundahar, 44, 75, 188
Gundioc, 75
Gundobad, 75, 190
Historia Brittonum, 21, 191
History of the Kings of Britain, 19, 27, 192, 203, 214
Hoard, 103
Hoël, 28, 29, 67
Holy Grail, 19, 24, 113
Homo Sapiens, 49, 195
Houac, 39
Isle of Apples, 46
Isle of Avalon, 29, 31, 32, 47, 56, 57, 59, 62, 63, 64, 65, 75, 96, 165
Isle of Glass, 63
Jacques-de-Compostelle, 38
Jersey, 64
Joseph of Arimathea, 64, 134, 175
Julius Caesar, 41, 102, 121, 178, 197, 198
Jupiter, 122, 126
King Budicius, 28
Knights of, 82
Knights Templar, 143, 157
Lancelot, 19, 63
Lazarus, 51, 133, 134
Le Corbusier, 114
Loire, 23, 36, 38, 102, 130, 155, 156
Lugudonum, 40
Lupus of Troyes, 131, 188
Magnance, 132
Magny, 123
Maine, 40
Malory, 20
Margam Abbey, 58
Mars, 102, 122, 124, 159
Marseilles, 134, 190
Martha, 133, 134
Martin de Tours, 129, 187
Mary Magdalene, 24, 51, 73, 89, 114, 115, 133, 134, 135, 165, 175, 192
Matter of Britain, 23, 83
Matter of France, 23, 82, 94

Mercury, 102, 121, 122, 123, 156, 159, 164
Merlin, 19, 27, 31, 65, 98, 106, 154, 201, 202
Meroveus, 36, 45, 189
Merovingian, 45, 125, 143, 149, 158, 162, 163, 164, 165, 170, 189, 190, 200
Minerva, 122, 123
Mithras, 104, 129
Montbard, 139
Montmarte, 102, 124, 125, 140, 178
Montréal, 139
Mont-Saint-Michel, 30
Mordred, 28, 30, 38, 56, 77, 150, 161, 180
Morgain, 64
Morgen le Fay, 17, 19, 28, 31, 46, 74, 75, 77, 80, 81, 180, 183
Morvan, 18, 49, 50, 51, 79, 102, 118, 148, 149, 150, 151, 153, 159, 160, 162, 169, 204, 206
Morvandus, 38, 78, 150, 161, 190
Mount Beuvray, 143, 159
Musée Archéologique de Dijon, 182
Museum of the Celts, 159
Narbonnais, 40
Nennius, 21, 161, 191
Neolithic, 24, 69, 82, 115, 139, 141, 152, 164, 195
Neustria, 40
Nîmes, 133
Normandy, 30, 40, 64, 142, 147
Nuars, 100
Obédiencérie, 166
Ouche, 177
Paladins, 82
Pallaye, 132
Paris (Lutècia), 148
Patrick, 61, 132, 187, 188, 189, 202
Pavia, 32
Pelagianism, 131, 188
Perceval, 64, 192
Picts, 29, 196
Pierre Perthuis, 70
Pontaubert, 156
Princess of Vix, 158
Quinotaur, 45

Ralph of Coggeshall, 58, 164
Reid, Howard, 205
Richard the Lionheart, 89, 108, 109, 110, 112
Riothamus, 15, 23, 34, 35, 36, 37, 38, 45, 47, 48, 50, 54, 62, 66, 67, 68, 73, 75, 77, 78, 81, 82, 95, 99, 107, 115, 117, 128, 129, 135, 145, 146, 149, 150, 156, 173, 175, 176, 178, 183, 190
Robert de Boron, 63, 64, 106, 192
Roches des Fées, 79
Roman de Brut, 64, 192, 206
Rome, 30, 131, 132, 143, 146, 150, 187, 188, 189, 190, 199, 200
Round Table, 19, 64, 82
Roy, Jules, 205
Sarmatians, 24, 103, 104, 105, 106
Saulieu, 143
Saxons, 29, 30, 35, 36, 57, 60, 98, 131, 188, 189, 190, 191, 196
Scots, 29, 196
Scythians, 105
Seine, 48, 84, 87, 89, 124, 136, 158, 168, 180, 181, 182, 191, 202
Sens (Agedincum), 50, 68
Sequani, 48
Sidonius, 36, 68, 175, 176, 188, 189, 190
Sociétié de Mythologie Française, 17, 78, 183
St. Germain des Champs, 148
St. Moré, 104, 123, 159, 162, 169, 170
St. Père-sous-Vézelay, 74, 87, 92
Stonehenge, 138, 154, 195
Syagrius, 36, 44, 45, 67, 68, 149, 173, 175, 190
Tennyson, 20
The Discovery of King Arthur, 15, 22, 34, 56, 151, 201, 214
The Knight of the Lion, 75
Third Crusade, 108, 109, 112, 167, 193
Thory, 126
Tor, 141
Touraine, 40
Troyes, 22, 39, 43, 63, 75, 88, 131, 188, 192, 205
Uther Pendragon, 27, 28, 40, 74, 97, 98, 99, 129, 154, 174, 188
Vales of Avalon, 64
Vault-de-Lugny, 156, 162
Vercingetorix, 49, 79, 102, 106, 125, 140, 178, 179, 198, 199
Via Agrippa, 38, 50, 68, 102, 103, 104, 118, 130, 132, 145, 148, 149, 158, 159

Via Lemovicensis, 38
Viollet-Le-Duc, 114
Visigoths, 35, 36, 37, 38, 43, 54, 66, 67, 78, 95, 145, 150, 188, 190, 191, 194
Vita Merlini, 19, 28, 31, 72, 76, 192
Vix Crater, 158
Vortigern, 97, 98, 131, 188, 189
Voutenay-sur-Cure, 104, 123, 162
Wace, 61, 64, 65, 180, 192, 206
Walter of Coventry, 109
Walter, Archdeacon of Oxford, 20
Wells Cathedral, 3, 166
William of Malmesbury, 145
William of Sens, 167, 192
Ygerna, 27, 135
Yonne, 48, 64, 89, 100, 103, 104, 131, 158, 162, 168, 204

ENDNOTES

[1] *Mythologie Francaise* Jean LALU 2003

[2] "There were mythical apple-islands in Welsh and Irish lore, Avallach and Ablach, and these have to be recognized. But Rachel Bromwich points out that Geoffrey's *Avallon* is NOT a Latinization of the Welsh Avallach and implies that something from Burgundy has found its way in. It looks as if he (Geoffrey of Monmouth) picked up a tradition of the real Avalon." Geoffrey Ashe, email to MF 26.04.07. Rachel Bromwich reference from *Trioedd Ynys Prydein: The Welsh Triads*, Cardiff, University of Wales Press, 2nd edition, 1978. Her reference to the Burgundian Avallon is on page 267

[3] In all research concerning Geoffrey of Monmouth's "The History of the Kings of Britain" I have used the Introduction and Translation by Lewis Thorpe in the Penguin Classics version first published in 1966

[4] Google.co.uk 2.11.07 web search

[5] Ibid

[6] Britannia History www.britannia.com

[7] Ibid

[8] The Discovery of King Arthur, Geoffrey Ashe, Sutton Publishing Edition 2003

[9] La Chanson de Girart de Roussillon. Traduction de Micheline de Combarieu du Grès et Gérard Gouiran Librairie Générale Française 1993

[10] My apologies to Geoffrey of Monmouth for summarising his writing – it does his work no justice – please read the whole book – version as above

[11] Ibid

[12] Ibid

[13] Both extracts from *Vita Merlini*, Geoffrey of Monmouth, translated by Emily Rebekah Huber at The Camelot Project, University of Rochester

[14] It is interesting to note that the first two places chosen by Geoffrey as an example of Morgen's shape-shifting abilities are in France. He also uses 'your shores' later in that paragraph which again suggests that her shores may be in foreign parts.

[15] There is another less-ancient village called 'Avalon' in the Isère Department, up in the French Alps. This is associated with Saint Hugh, who became Bishop of Lincoln, and Château Bayard (circa 15 century).

[16] *The Discovery of King Arthur* Geoffrey Ashe 2003 Sutton Publishing England.

[17] Ibid

[18] Ibid

[19] Ibid

[20] Ibid

[21] Ibid

[22] Ibid

[23] Guide de la Bourgogne et du Lyonnais Mystérieux, Patrice BOUSSEL, les Guides Noirs Editions Tchou Princesse 1978

[24] ibid.

[25] Carte Archéologique de la France – L'Yonne Jean-Paul Delor

[26] AVALLON ANCIEN ET MODERNE A. Heurley Imprime L.BARRE, Place-St Julien 1880

[27] "It strikes me as significant that when Glastonbury claimed to have the bones of St. Dunstan, Canterbury hotly denied it with a counter-claim, and there was quite a dispute. The Arthur discovery was in sharp contrast. I don't think anybody challenged it for centuries, and no rival grave was ever produced, even in Wales." Geoffrey Ashe, email to MF 27 June 2008

[28] ARTHURIAN ROMANCES Erec and Enide trans. Carleton W. Carrol 1991 Penguin Books

[29] MERLIN AND THE GRAIL Trilogy of Arthurian Romances Trans. Nigel Bryant 2001 Boydell & Brewer Ltd

[30] Translated by Dell Skeels ARTHURIAN CHRONICLES ROMAN DE BRUT Trans Eugene Mason Kessinger Publishing
[31] Ibid
[32] The Discovery of King Arthur, Geoffrey ASHE, Sutton Publishing 2005
[33] 'Les Fontaines Salées Vézelay gallo-romain' Francois VOGARDE 1980 Magasin St-Bernard VEZELAY
[34] Histoire de Vézelay, Bernard PUJO, 2000 Librarie Academique Perrin
[35] Ibid Pierre-Perthuis
[36] Gerald never misses an opportunity to get it in again
[37] Le Site Sacré de Vézelay BONNET Editions J. Bonnet 42300 Roanne
[38] Les Fontaines Salées, François VOGARDE Magasin St-Bernard VEZELAY 1980
[39] LA CHANSON DE GIRART DE ROUSSILLON anon. translation & notes Micheline de Combarieu du Gres & Derard Gouiran 1993 Le Livre de Poche <Lettres Gothiques
[40] Carte Archéologique de la Gaule – l'Yonne 89/2 Jean-Paul Delor
[41] Charter 1 from the Cartulary of the Vézelay Chronicle by Hugh of Poitiers, by John Scott and John O. Ward 1992 Medieval & Renaissance Texts and Studies, Binghamton, New York
[42] LA CHANSON DE GIRART DE ROUSSILLON anon. translation & notes Micheline de Combarieu du Gres & Derard Gouiran 1993 Le Livre de Poche <Lettres Gothiques
[43] Ibid
[44] Avallon et l'Avallonnais, Ernest Petit
[45] Ibid
[46] Ibid
[47] Histoire de Vézelay, Bernard Pujo 2000 Librairie Academique Perrin
[48] LA CHANSON DE GIRART DE ROUSSILLON
[49] Ibid
[50] The History of the Kings of Britain

[51] Ibid
[52] Ibid
[53] Ibid
[54] Histoire de Vezelay, Bernard Pujo 2000 Librairie Académique Perrin
[55] Carte Archeologique de la Gaule – l'Yonne 89/2 Jean-Paul Delor
[56] avallon.info/avallonnais-gallo-romain/avl_fontenay.htm
[57] Carte Archeologique de la Gaule – l'Yonne 89/2 Jean-Paul Delor
[58] Ibid
[59] Carte Archeologique de la Gaule – l'Yonne 89/2 Jean-Paul Delor
[60] Arthur the Dragon King, Howard Reid, Headline Book Publishing, London 2001
[61] King Arthur in Combat, Robert de Boron. L'Estoire de Merlin. Bibliotheque nationale, Paris, France.
[62] Geoffrey of Monmouth's "The History of the Kings of Britain"Introduction and Translation by Lewis Thorpe in the Penguin Classics version first published in 1966
[63] Roger of Hoveden Vol 2
[64] Extract from a letter by Guy de Bazoches cited in Histoire de Vezelay, Bernard Pujo 2000 Librairie Académique Perrin
[65] VEZELAY – A sentimental Guide 1995 L'Or des Etoiles, Jules ROY Trans. Georges Michel, Nicole and Larry Mallet
[66] GLASTONBURY, Avalon of the Heart, Dion Fortune 1995 Weiser Books, York Beach Maine USA
[67] Carte Archéologique de la Gaule L'Yonne 89/2
[68] The Archaeological Museum in Dijon, the Museum at Châtillon-sur-Seine and The Museum of Celtic Civilization, Bibracte, contain the extensive finds from these shrines.
[69] Carte Archéologique de la Gaule L'Yonne 89/2
[70] Dictionary of Celtic Myth and Legend, Miranda GREEN Thames and Hudson 1992
[71] Carte Archéologique de la Gaule L'Yonne 89/2

[72] Avallon Ancien et Moderne A. Heurley 1880 Librairie Voillot Avallon

[73] De Bello Gallico VI, 14 cited in The Druids, T.D.Kendrick Methuen & Co London 1927

[74] Ibid

[75] Avallon et Avallonnais, Ernest Petit Librairie Voillot, Avallon 1867

[76] J. Gaudemet, Les canons des conciles mérovingiens (Vie – VIIe siècles), Sources Chrétiennes, 353 et 354 Paris 1989 (traduction J. Gaudemet)

[77] The Vézelay Chronicle, Hugh of Poitiers, Trans John Scottand John O. Ward, Center for Medieval Studies, State University of New York 1992

[78] The Vézelay Chronicle, Hugh of Poitiers, transl. John SCOTT and John O. WARD Pegasus Paperbooks, New York 1992

[79] Bloodline of the Holy Grail, Sir Laurence GARDNER

[80] Une Demeure Alchimique le Château de Chastenay, Gabrielde LA VARENDE Editions du Chastenay 1990, ISBN 2 908 772 00 0

[81] Un Peuple de Pelerins, Offrandes de pierre et de bronze des Sources de la Seine, Simone DEYTS, Dijon 1994

[82] Cart Archaeologique de la Gaule, L'Yonne 89/2 Jean-Paul Delor 2002

[83] Ibid

[84] Vézelay Symbolisme et Esotérisme, François VOGADE, Guillaudot varennes-Vauzelles 1998

[85] The History of the Kings of Britain, Geoffrey of Monmouth Trans. Lewis THORPE Penguin Classics 1966

[86] Cambridge University Library MS 1706

[87] The Discovery of King Arthur, Geoffrey ASHE, Sutton Publishing 2005

[88] Ibid

[89] Villes et Campagnes du Departement de L'Yonne – Arrondissement d'Avallon PETIT Victor, Librairie Voillot, Avallon 2001 reprint of Gallot, Auxerre, 1870

[90] Carte Archéologique de la Gaule, L'Yonne 89/2 Jean-Pail DELOR 2002
[91] Ibid
[92] Villes et Campagnes du Departement de L'Yonne – Arrondissement d'Avallon PETIT Victor, Librarie Voillot, Avallon 2001 reprint of Gallot, Auxerre, 1870
[93] Carte Archeologique de la Gaule, L'Yonne 89/2 Jean-Pail DELOR 2002
[94] Villes et Campagnes du Departement de L'Yonne – Arrondissement d'Avallon PETIT Victor, Librarie Voillot, Avallon 2001 reprint of Gallot, Auxerre, 1870
[95] Carte Archeologique de la Gaule, L'Yonne 89/2 Jean-Pail DELOR 2002
[96] Ibid
[97] Ibid
[98] Ibid
[99] Ibid
[100] History of the Franks, GREGORY OF TOURS